ANALYS

90 0898612 X

J EDUCATION IN
ZAMBIA

D1765744

Peter Matimba

ANALYSIS OF IMPACT OF HIV ON CHILDREN'S EDUCATION IN ZAMBIA

Strategies, Effectiveness and Sustainability of Interventional Models in Zambia

VDM Verlag Dr. Müller

Impressum/Imprint (nur für Deutschland/ only for Germany)

Bibliografische Information der Deutschen Nationalbibliothek: Die Deutsche Nationalbibliothek verzeichnet diese Publikation in der Deutschen Nationalbibliografie; detaillierte bibliografische Daten sind im Internet über http://dnb.d-nb.de abrufbar.
Alle in diesem Buch genannten Marken und Produktnamen unterliegen warenzeichen-, marken- oder patentrechtlichem Schutz bzw. sind Warenzeichen oder eingetragene Warenzeichen der jeweiligen Inhaber. Die Wiedergabe von Marken, Produktnamen, Gebrauchsnamen, Handelsnamen, Warenbezeichnungen u.s.w. in diesem Werk berechtigt auch ohne besondere Kennzeichnung nicht zu der Annahme, dass solche Namen im Sinne der Warenzeichen- und Markenschutzgesetzgebung als frei zu betrachten wären und daher von jedermann benutzt werden dürften.

Coverbild: www.purestockx.com

Verlag: VDM Verlag Dr. Müller Aktiengesellschaft & Co. KG
Dudweiler Landstr. 99, 66123 Saarbrücken, Deutschland
Telefon +49 681 9100-698, Telefax +49 681 9100-988, Email: info@vdm-verlag.de
Zugl.: Zambia, Cavendish University, Diss 2008

Herstellung in Deutschland:
Schaltungsdienst Lange o.H.G., Berlin
Books on Demand GmbH, Norderstedt
Reha GmbH, Saarbrücken
Amazon Distribution GmbH, Leipzig
ISBN: 978-3-639-21049-1

Imprint (only for USA, GB)

Bibliographic information published by the Deutsche Nationalbibliothek: The Deutsche Nationalbibliothek lists this publication in the Deutsche Nationalbibliografie; detailed bibliographic data are available in the Internet at http://dnb.d-nb.de .
Any brand names and product names mentioned in this book are subject to trademark, brand or patent protection and are trademarks or registered trademarks of their respective holders. The use of brand names, product names, common names, trade names, product descriptions etc. even without a particular marking in this works is in no way to be construed to mean that such names may be regarded as unrestricted in respect of trademark and brand protection legislation and could thus be used by anyone.

Cover image: www.purestockx.com

Publisher:
VDM Verlag Dr. Müller Aktiengesellschaft & Co. KG
Dudweiler Landstr. 99, 66123 Saarbrücken, Germany
Phone +49 681 9100-698, Fax +49 681 9100-988, Email: info@vdm-publishing.com

Printed in the U.S.A.
Printed in the U.K. by (see last page)
ISBN: 978-3-639-21049-1

TABLE OF CONTENTS

ACRONYMS

ACRWC - African Charter on the Rights and Welfare of a Child

ANPPCAN – African Network for Prevention and Protection against Child Abuse and Neglect

AIDS - Acquired Immune Deficiency Syndrome

CAA - Catholic AIDS Action

CHANGES- Community Health And Nutrition Gender Education Services

CHEP -Copperbelt Health Education Project

CIC - Children In Crisis

COPE-Community-based   Options   for   the   Protection   and   Empowerment

CSO – Central Statistical Office

CYC- Community Youth Concern

CWACs - Community Welfare Assistance Committees

DEBS - District Education Boards

EFA – Education For All

EMIS - Education Management Information System

FAWEZA- Forum for Women Educationist in Zambia

FBE - Free Basic Education

FBOs – Faith based Organisations

FNDP - Fifth National Development Plan

GDP - Gross Domestic Product

GRZ – Government of Republic of Zambia

HDR – Human Development Report

HIV - Human Immune Virus

IEC – Information, Education, and Communication

IGA – Income generating Activity

ILO - International Labour Organisation

JCTR -Jesuit Centre for Theological Reflection

KCM - Konkola Copper Mines

MCDSS - Ministry of Community Development and Social Services

MDG – Millennium Development Goals

MFNP – Ministry of Finance and National Planning

MLSS - Ministry of labour and Social Security

MMD – Movement for Multiparty Democracy

MoU- Memorandum of Understanding

MoE – Ministry of Education

MVCs - Most Vulnerable Committees

MYSCD- Ministry of Youth, Sports and Child Development

NAC - National AIDS Council

NGOs - Non Governmental Organisations

NPA - National Plan of Action

OVCs – Orphans and other Vulnerable Children

PCI - Project Concern International

PTA - Parent Teachers' Association

PWAS -Public Welfare Assistance Schemes

UN CRC - United Nations Charter on the Right of a Child

UNGAS – United Nations General Assembly Special Report on AIDS

UNZA – University of Zambia

USAID - United States Agency for International Development

USA – United States of America

SCU – Save the Children UK

SCS – Save the Children Sweden

WPF – World Population Foundation

WFCL - Worst Forms of Child Labour

ZANEC - Zambia National Educational Coalition

ZARAN -Zambia AIDSLaw and Research Network

ZCEA - Zambia Civic Education Association

ZCSS - Zambia Community Schools Secretariat

ZCTU - Zambia Congress of Trade Unions

ZFE - Zambia Federation of Employees

ZMK – Zambian Kwacha

ZRCS - Zambia Red Cross Society

ACKNOWLEDGEMENTS

Each journey begins with one step! I took my first step in April 2006 when I began written this book project. It has been a long, bumpy and challenging journey, but has been worth taking. To those I talked and walked the journey with, you are great people! I am so grateful for your courage and determination. The journey has been full of sacrifice and to you, I am so indebted. Some of you are fathers, mothers, and above all, captains of industries but you still took time off your busy schedules to walk with me. I am also indebted to a number of individuals and institutions for contributions they rendered to see this book project to completion.

My sincere gratitude also goes to my members of staff for their encouragement and input into this book project. My special appreciation goes to Ejang, Parsley and Peace, Jacqueline, and Matacks and Family, without you, the journey could have been lonely and difficult. You are great people and you will always be a blessing to me.

DEDICATION

I dedicate this Project Book to God. You are the Pillar of my Life and Destiny! Without you, the world would have missed my contribution towards equitable socio-economic justice for mankind.

I THANK, YOU ALL

CHAPTER 1

1.0   INTRODUCTION AND BACKGROUND

1.1   INTRODUCTION

In this chapter, I indicate and analyse objectives of the research. Specifically, the research critically analyses effectiveness and sustainability of educational models in mitigating impact of HIV on children in Zambia, a case study carried out in four (4) communities in Lusaka district, Zambia. In addition, I will further outline positive impact and contributions by government and non-state actors in the fight against HIV and how such interventional models positively and sustainably respond to educational needs of children affected by the pandemic.

1.2   PROBLEM BACKGROUND

The HIV pandemic is causing socio-economic among vulnerable households. Coupled with poverty, child labour and reduced extended family cohesion, HIV is a threat to a health world population. Denis Wood indicates that the prevalence and severity of HIV fuels the dramatic increase in levels of child mortality rates and this has further resulted into the increase in the number of orphans affected by the pandemic (Save the Children Sweden, 2008). It can be inferred that HIV affects Zambia's attainment of MDG No. 4, which seeks to reduce child mortality rates by 2015.

The estimates on total number of orphans affected and infected by HIV in Zambia differ depending on the source. The UNAIDS Report indicates that of the 15,200,000 children orphaned by HIV globally as at 2005, about 12,000,000 of these children come from Sub-Saharan region (UNAIDS Report on Global AIDS Epidemic, May 2006). Doek, former UN Committee Chairperson on the rights of the child indicates that more than 25 million people globally are living with the virus and also that HIV is the leading cause of death in Africa. He further indicates that about 22 million children under the age of 18 years have lost one of both parents (Doek, 2007) and Sub Sahara Africa remains the region worst affected by HIV representing two – thirds (2/3) of globally affected people. Further, Doek indicates that the epidemic impacts negatively on the daily lives of younger children and exposes their victimisation and marginalisation, especially those living in difficult circumstances.

1

The data from the Living Conditions Monitoring Survey for 2005 suggests that of the 1,197,867 total number of vulnerable children (OVCs), at least 598,932 are directly affected by HIV pandemic (CSO,2005). In addition, the number of children orphaned by the HIV has increased to from 598,932 in 2005 to 801,420 as 2008 (UNGASS[1], 2008 and HDR 2007)[2]. From these estimates, Zambia represents 5% of the 12,160,516 people as the number of children affected by HIV in the Sub-Saharan region. In terms of infection, the UNAIDS Report estimates that there are at least 1,500,000 in sub-Saharan region and 1,700,000 globally are children from 0 to 14 years.

Many people argue that the unprecedented problem of HIV and number of orphans may affect Zambia's population growth including reservoir of future leadership. It is for this reason that many sections of society have taken both preventive and remedial actions to respond to this devastating impact of the pandemic.

One area that this research will also assess in detail is positive impact, responsiveness and sustainability of interventional support towards educational needs of children affected by HIV pandemic. To date, many players have used different models and approaches to respond to HIV and educational is one such model. Through this research activity, I will critically analyse effectiveness and sustainability of educational models in mitigating impact of HIV on children in Zambia conducted in 4 study communities, namely Matero, Chunga, Chaisa and George in Lusaka District, Zambia.

1.3   SIGNIFICANCE OF THE RESEARCH
Education is long term investment that every child must enjoy for personal mental growth and national socio-economic development. Factors that threaten the provision and access to education must be researched and understood so that preventive and remedial policies and activities are put in place by the various stakeholders The National Child Policy of Zambia underscores the importance of education because education enables them, among other things to

---

[1] UNGASS - United Nation General Assembly Special Session (2008)
[2] HDR - Human Development Report (2007)

interact with fellow children and also empowers them socio-economically to reduce their vulnerability to exploitation (GRZ, 2006).

With adequate education, children in their childhood and also when they become socio-economically empowered can protect themselves from to poverty, HIV, child labour and other forms of violence. The United Nations Charter on the Right of a Child (UN CRC, 1989) also provides that all children have the right to access basic and quality education. In addition, though the UN CRC mentioned above does not contain a specific provision addressing the prevention and treatment of HIV, article 24 and 28 provide for the right to enjoy the highest attainable standard of health education respectively (Doek, 2007). In addition, the Millennium Development Goal (MDG 2) provides for university access to basic education for children by 2015.

On the other hand, though the Zambian constitution provides that the right to education is not an enforceable once denied by government or any other stakeholder, through international human rights instruments and local policies, the government has certain policies that promote children's access to education. The Educational Policy provides that government as custodian of human rights of all individuals, including their right to education takes necessary steps to make education accessible by children in the school going age (MoE, 1996).

This research seeks to assess impact of HIV and sustainability of educational support models towards children's access to education. The research highlights current opportunities and problems that facilitates and or hinder effective prevention and mitigation of HIV by the various models. It further suggests how opportunities and gaps can be prudently managed in view of limited financial and human resource.

1.4   OBJECTIVES OF THE BOOK PROJECT

1.4.1   To assess the negative impact of HIV on educational opportunities for children in four (4) communities in Lusaka, Zambia

1.4.2   To assess the effectiveness of preventive and remedial strategies by government and non-state actors in Zambia.

3

1.4.3 To assess sustainability of educational models in managing HIV among children in 4 communities in Lusaka, Zambia

1.4.4 To identify good practices positively responds to HIV impact in 4 communities in Lusaka, Zambia

1.5 PROBLEM STATEMENT

The HIV pandemic affects children in Zambia. It results into among others, loss of life, and denies them natural care and support from their biological parents and close family members. HIV also denies them access to educational opportunities. The preventive and remedial approaches aimed at responding to educational needs of children affected by HIV are inadequate and rarely sustainable.

I feel that in spite of the large financial and expertise investments made by various stakeholders, HIV has continued to infect and affect adults and children not only in Zambia but globally with Sub Sahara Africa is deemed to be the most hit. Probably the models used lack practical impact and this may also affect the sustainability of gains achieved. UNICEF and UNAIDS "Call to Action" Report indicates that every day;

- There are nearly 1,800 new infections in children under 15 mostly from mother to child transmission
- 1,400 children under 15 years die of HIV and AIDS related illness
- More than 6,000 young people aged 15 – 24 are newly infected with HIV

BUT after more than 20 years of the epidemic,

- Less than 10% of pregnant women are being offered service to prevent transmission of the HIV to their infants
- Less than 10% of the children who have been orphaned or made vulnerable by HIV and AIDS receive public support services
- Less than one third (1/3) of the young women aged 15 – 24 in sub-Saharan Africa fully understand how to avoid the disease ((2006:2).

1.6 RESEARCH QUESTIONS

1.6.1 Does HIV have any negative impact on educational opportunities for children?

4

1.6.2 Do government policies and non state actor interventions reduce negative impact of HIV on children and increase their educational opportunities?

1.6.3 How responsive and sustainable are the available government policies and interventions of non-state actors?

1.6.4 Are there any documented practices that have demonstrated positive contribution to reducing negative impact of HIV in general and improve in educational opportunities for children in particular?

1.7 FORMAT OF THE RESEARCH

The research contains six chapters. Chapter one is research problem background, objectives, and problem statement as well as the research questions. Chapter two contains literature review. It is followed by chapter three, which outlines the research methodology. This is followed by chapter four, which presents findings of the research. Chapter five discusses and interprets research findings. Finally, the research ends with chapter six, which concludes and also provides recommendations of the study to key stakeholders.

1.8 OVERVIEW AND IMPACT OF HIV PANDEMIC

The HIV pandemic is most prevalent among the productive age groups. Inevitably, this has negative implication on demographic and socio-economic development in terms of population growth and delivery of social services. Because of inadequate educational skills, such children and youths are likely to be less competitive and productive in the labour market and industries respectively.

The tables 1.8.1 and 1.8.2 below gives an overview of impact of HIV on productive age groups in global and Sub-Saharan regions as obtained from UNAIDS Report on Global AIDS Epidemic (May 2006).

Table 1.8.1:   Infection rates of HIV among the productive age groups

Region	0-14 (in years)	15 -24 (in years)
Global	3,500,000	4,300,000
Sub-Saharan	3,000,000	5,100,000
Total	**6,500,000**	**9,400,000**

Table 1.8.2:   Death estimates due to HIV illness and Number of HIV affected orphans

Region	Number of people died of HIV related illness	Children orphaned by HIV
Global	3,300,000	15,000,000
Sub Saharan	2,300,000	12,000,0000
Total	**5,600,000**	**27,000,000**

In addition, HIV leads to many orphaned children left too young to care for themselves. As a result, many end up organised child headed households especially that there is an erosion of extended family safety nets. The ILO training manual on Child labour and HIV and AIDS also reveals that the extended family networks has played a major role in absorbing children orphaned by HIV pandemic and those left out of extended family safety nets end up engaging in worst forms of child labour (ILO-IPEC 2006:57).

The government policy on free education is not practical as such. The free educational policy that allows free basic education for all Zambian children until the ninth grade is not practically free because children still pay user fees to facilitate school operational costs. The fees are beyond what many households are able to pay. Denis Wood in his research, notes that despite the Free Basic Education Policy, one HIV affected widow in Western Province of Zambia was found spending one hundred and twenty thousand Zambian Kwacha (ZMK 120,000.00) per term per child to cover the cost of school uniforms, transport, school bags, shoes, PTA fees and other school related incidentals (Save the Children Sweden, 2008).

In addition, lack of access to quality education is felt through negative impact on the mental development of an individual child. This may further limit children's capacity to explore

6

scientific skills and knowledge for practical transformation into products and services for market consumption. The UN CRC, 1989 also indicates that lack of education opportunities limits children's ability to develop their personal talents and level of contribution towards the needs and expectations of society (UN CRC, 1989:6).

The spread of HIV in Zambia has been very fast, starting from early 1980s when the first case was diagnosed in Zambia. By 1985, HIV cases reached 629, and by 2005, the infection rate was at 44,329 while people living with HIV in the same year were 914,691. In addition, by 2005, there were 801,420 children orphaned by HIV while people dying of HIV related illness stood at 489,330 (UNGASS Report 2008 and HDR 2007)

1.9   IMPACT OF HIV ON QUALITY OF EDUCATION

HIV and AIDS affect children indirectly and directly when nursing chronically ill parents/bread winners and also when they lose parents/ breadwinners. This equally increases the demand for care and other basic services.   HIV pandemic affect steady progress rates at which the developing countries are moving towards attainment of MDG bench marks (HDR, 2007).

Former UN Secretary General Koffi Annan also notes that HIV affects progress in attaining other MDGs and had this to say, 'How we fare in the fight against HIV is crucial. Halting the spread is not only an MDG itself; it is a pre-requisite for reaching most of others. Only if we meet this challenge can we succeed in our efforts to build a humane, healthy and equitable world. Let us ensure we are equal to it (UNGASS Report 2008).

1.10   STAKEHOLDERS IN MITIGATING HIV PANDEMIC

As the former UN Committee on the Rights of a Child puts it, 'HIV and AIDS is not a problem of some countries and individuals but of the entire world and to bring this negative impact on children under control will require concerted and well targeted efforts from all countries at all levels of development and interventions (Doek, 2007).

1.10.1 The Role of Government

In any market driven economy, government is responsible for policy formulation and enforcement while service delivery is open to private sector, development organisations, and stakeholders. UN CRC (1989) also suggests that the professional and practical response to the plights of children infected and or affected by HIV and AIDS depends on the quality of policies put in place and implemented by governments (Doek, 2007).

Even in the early years of the third republic (1991), government had already seen the importance of other stakeholders. Invitations to non-state actors to partner with government in providing quality education were extended to them due to increase cost of education and fees which the government alone could not afford (Carmody, 2004).

In addition, the decline in socio-economic performance in the 1980s resulted into shrinking of resources. Therefore, educational sector no long received the kind of budget allocation that was needed to maintain as well as expanding the system. This was further affected by the rapid increase in population from three million and five hundred (3,500,000) in 1968 to about twelve million one hundred and sixty thousand five hundred and sixteen (12,160,516) today. This presents a growth % of over 3% per annum.

On the other hand, the period 1970s and 1980s saw the allocation of resources to the education sector shifting to university education while primary, secondary, teacher training and technical education saw a major decline. According to Carmody, the unit of primary education fell by 25% and by over 50% for secondary education while the same rose by over 40% at university level in the period 1975 to 1985.

The aforementioned scenario compelled the government to come up with adjustment measures, which included the decentralisation of the education system. This enabled participation of more non-state partners in educational infrastructure development and service provision. This opened up means and ways for construction of basic schools by local communities and giving more attractive conditions to grant-aided and private schools (Carmody, 2004).

With the dwindling of government resource base against increasing and competing demands, government had to invite other stakeholders to supplement its efforts to reach out children and communities where its systems may not adequately serve. According to National Educational Policy, effective partnership with other stakeholders in educational provision is vital (MoE, 1996). In addition, the current MoE National Implementation Framework for 2008 to 2010 provides for development of a mechanism that engages government with private sector and development organisations in education service provision. At global level too, the Zambian government's commitment can be reflected in its party to declaration and provisions of the 8 MDGs and other international instruments.

1.10.2 The Role of Development Organisations and other Stakeholders

The development organisations and play a critical role in addressing the impact of HIV and AIDS among children. ILO-IPEC (2006:66), also underscores the role of coordinated efforts of various stakeholders towards elimination of HIV and AIDS impact on children through provision of services as a common front and alliance. Doek also believes that non state actors such as development organisations and religious leaders can play an important role in terms of awareness raising and prevention (UNICEF, 2004).

Education has been one of the most frequently used models and strategies to addressing HIV and AIDS impact. It is believed that education can play major roles in reducing immediate and long-term impact. They target children infected and or affected through project and program based approach funded from internal and external sources.

In Zambia, there is no universally accepted and or agreed model. Hence, development organisations and other non state stakeholders use different models to enhance children's opportunities to education. The activities, projects and programs differ from organisation to organisation and at times from one project to another within the same organisation and or donor. Mostly, the support given range from infrastructure development, provision of scholastic materials, nutrition, payment of school fees/bursaries, provision of school uniforms and teaching materials to training to teachers.

9

Unlike the private sector that uses resources from their corporate social responsibility volts, the majority of development organisations and other community response mechanisms to HIV and AIDS projects and programs use external funds from donors. These funds always have known limited and short timeframes after which, funding may exhaust or the project closes. In terms of sustaining the gains, most of interventions are time bound and donor dependant. For instance, activities, projects and programs have an average of months to 1-3 years, a period which is far much shorter than the number of years a child needs to start school and complete basic education.

1.11   COMPETITIVENESS OF STRATEGIES

It is believed that the increase in HIV and AIDS infection and prevalence since early 1990s and onwards led to quick mushrooming of non- state actors in Zambia and elsewhere. At the same time, community response mechanisms also emerged to provide services to children orphaned that could not be taken in by the declining extended family safety nets. In terms of targeting and efficiency, development organisations and community response mechanisms have a competitive edge as compared to bureaucratic government service delivery systems.

Further, the development organisations and community response mechanism could have made quick inroads in responding to the needs of affected children probably due to their specific targets and specialisation compared to government systems of services delivery. Unlike government, the development organisations and other stakeholders address identifiable problems with specific budgets and timeframes. This means that human, financial and materials resources are spent on addressing a specific problem. Once this problem has been addressed, the attention and priority may immediately shift to other equally vulnerable beneficiaries within or to another community. As a result, there is certainly revolving capacity and skills in specific areas of their interest by development organisations and other actors.

For instance, in 2002, Save the Children United Kingdom (SC UK) carried out a research in Somali to identify the various categories of children excluded from formal school systems and the reasons for their exclusion. After the research, specific, responsive and alternative basic education delivery mechanisms, compatible with the problem and environment were designed.

10

Targeting children from approximately over 70% of pastoralist and migrants coupled with child labour were discovered to be among the major problems affecting children's access to basic education in Somali (SC UK, 2007).

In response, SC UK piloted mobile schools in 15 villages each having one permanent structure and two satellite sites so that children remaining in homes could attend permanent structure schools while those in the grazing pastures attend the satellite schools (SC UK 2007). To enhance continuation and sustainability, SC UK also trained local teachers and school committees to deliver quality lessons and provide management guidance respectively. The aforementioned are some of competitive edges of non state actors' approaches over government delivery systems. If the problem that SC UK was concerned about in Somali was impact of HIV and AIDS on education of the children of pastoralist and migrants through evidence-based research, this could have been established. Then a compatible project could have been developed to address the impact of HIV and AIDS on children of the pastoralists and migrants.

1.12 SUSTAINABILITY OF HIV INTERVENTIONAL APPROACHES

In 1990s, development organisations and other actors have emerged to prevent and address the impact of HIV and AIDS among different target groups in Zambia. However, many HIV and AIDS intervention models lack successful past precedence. Though some may have partially and or completely worked in other continents, countries and communities, they may not work in all parts of Zambia due differences in social status, nutrition, social infrastructures, attitudes, awareness, educational and knowledge among others.

In view of this, it is important to assess how a project is likely to sustain itself or how the promoters including the beneficiaries envisage the issue of sustainability. In any intervention, it must be clear on how services to beneficiaries upon the exhaustion of available external resources may continue. This should be clear and well understood by all those involved in the project management and service delivery at all levels.

1.13   SUMMARY OF THE CHAPTER

From the discussion in this chapter, it is evident that HIV is a multi-dimensional problem that has devastating effect on the overall society and educational opportunities for children. Further, the effect of HIV on family members affects children in many aspects of life. Many children miss education because HIV coupled with the high poverty levels reduces household incomes due to deaths and chronic illness of breadwinners. Apart from reduced chances of attending school, some become breadwinners and end up engaging in dangerous and hazardous works such as early marriages, having elderly men as boy friends including working in homes and other unsafe public places that increase their vulnerability to HIV pandemic. Further, its spread has negative impact on national socio-economic productivity, growth and development.

In addition, government is mandated to provide policies and social services to its citizens including providing opportunities for children to access education. Government has shown local and international commitment to promote to increase children's access to education through educational polices and international instruments (UN CRC, 1989). In addition, government's commitments towards education is reflected in 8 MDGs on Universal Education, elimination of poverty, reducing HIV and AIDS infection and others by 2015. Further, through EFA, government abolished statutory school fees and uniforms to fulfill national and international commitments to destroy any barrier that may hinder children's access and completion of basic education.

However, education is far from being free in Zambia. Children still pay in form of user fees and other operational costs. On the other hand, government is increasingly encouraging the participation of other stakeholders in HIV and AIDS mitigation and investment in educating children in general and those affected in particular. This is in line with international development agenda that also encourages inclusion of all stakeholders in educational service delivery and investments.

However, mere provision of educational support services and its short term impact on recipients alone does not address long term impact of HIV pandemic. Therefore, the issue of sustainability of models remains a concern because only practical and sustainable models may significantly reduce HIV impact.

It can be reiterated that education is an important tool for reducing multiple causal and impact of HIV among children and all sectors of the economy. However, this requires concerted and coordinated efforts by governments, development partners, communities and beneficiaries among others.

CHAPTER 2

2.0   LITERATURE REVIEW

2.1   INTRODUCTION

In this chapter, I look at some of the conventions and policies that government uses to address the impact of HIV pandemic to realise children's to education in Zambia. Secondly, I also analyse the impact of educational models that non state actors use to address the HIV impact among children and other vulnerable groups in society. Thirdly, the chapter also analyses the sustainability of policies, conventions and interventional models in view of inadequate resource bases Vs increasing demand for educational and other social services by children and households affected and those at risk of HIV pandemic.

2.2   HIV AND CAUSAL FACTORS

2.2.1   Household Poverty Levels

Many documented literatures indicate that poverty is linked directly as well as indirectly to the spread of HIV pandemic in society. Inadequate household income and chronic illness, poor medical services and deaths of breadwinners, inevitably affect children's access, and completion of basic education. When people become poor, they become more vulnerable to HIV infection and do not live longer after the diagnosis, as is the case with a wealth HIV infected person. Dr. Kenneth Kaunda suggests that HIV and AIDS can easily be defeated if poverty is eradicated (Chanda, 2008).

Therefore, households with inadequate incomes become more vulnerable to further impact of HIV and AIDS especially when breadwinners become chronically ill and or die. According to the Living Conditions Monitoring Survey, Lusaka District accounted for 57.8% of the total number of children affected by HIV and AIDS (CSO, 2004). This % is high and it goes without saying that children from these households lack access to education, food, clothing and other basic essentials like healthcare in Lusaka District.

14

In Zambia, the rapid spread of HIV can be directly linked to poor performance of the economy and effects of the privatisation outcomes. This is so because at a time the first case of HIV was diagnosed in 1984, it was at the very time Zambia's socio-economic performance was doing very badly with poverty levels around 85%. Inevitably, the call for a shift from socially to market driven economy was seen as an option.

2.2.2 Inadequate Social Protection Safety Nets

Prior to emergence of HIV, there were no terms like orphaned and other vulnerable children (OVCs) as well as child headed households because extended families had strong coping mechanisms to take in children left upon deaths of parents and other breadwinners. However, the spread of HIV and its socio-economic impact in the last 25 years has destroyed the once strong extended family safety nets and social cohesion networks. As a result, children are no longer left in the hands of extended families and as a result, they find themselves with little chance of care and support within extended families. Unfortunately, this lack of extended family and other coping mechanisms make orphaned children extremely vulnerable to HIV infection, child labour, and other hazardous and child unfriendly working environments.

Dr. Kaunda suggests as of 2003, which is 20 years after the first case was diagnosed, HIV prevalence estimates stood at 20%. In addition, nearly 200 people in productive age groups are buried on a daily basis, leaving many orphaned children without care and support apart from a few being cared for by communities, development organisations and extended family members (Care International Bulletin, 2003).

According to Children In Crisis (CIC), the HIV will continue to breed the social impact of OVCs in Zambia. These children require concerted efforts from government, development organisations, communities, private sector and other stakeholders providing essential services including education (CIC, bulletin, 2007).

07).

Though some children can afford to work and also go to school, their performance is unlikely to match with other children because the former lack adequate study time and even time to

15

consistently attend school. Their attendance and concentration in school is affected by increased demand for survival work, which are normally domestic work, garden work, vending among others. Some studies that have been conducted by some child rights organisations show that the majority of the children working as domestic workers as well as being in school do not manage to continue with and complete their basic education whilst working (Footprint Report, 2002:18).

This shows a close relationship between poverty and HIV because most of the children working as domestic workers as well as being in school including those who have dropped out of school can be attributed to reduced household incomes upon deaths of breadwinners due to HIV related deaths. On the other hand, though there is a reduction in social protection safety nets especially the extended family one, the demand for essential services from children and households keeps on increasing due to poverty and HIV and AIDS pandemic.

2.2.3   Effects of Privatisation on Household Incomes

The privatisation policy that Zambia embraced in the early 1990s entails a shift from socially regulated economy to market-driven economy. The immediate effects of the new economic management among others were restructuring and down sizing of companies through redundancies and retrenchments. This resulted into job losses and mass unemployment because new company and businesses owners only wanted few but competent staff in their new acquired companies. Unfortunately, these changes have negative financial implication on individual and households of retrenches and retirees. It also affects provision of adequate essential services to households including children's education due to reduced or complete lack of household incomes.

As though this was not bad enough, Zambia's shift from socially regulated economy to market driven economy took place in 1990s, almost the same time HIV pandemic began to spread rapidly. With reduced incomes, it was obvious that many retrenches, retirees and their immediate family members and other extended families who were beneficiaries became more vulnerable to combined forces of HIV and poverty.

16

The ultimate products of the aforementioned scenarios discussed earlier are accelerated rates at which HIV pandemic spread and also the increase in the number of orphaned children who require care and support for essential services.

2.3   THE HIV AND AIDS IMPACT ON EDUCATION

The unprecedented impact of the HIV pandemic affects children's access to and completion of basic education in Zambia. Many children drop out of school to engage into work and other means of survival. Equally, many are unlikely to start school because the caregivers and or the households they stay in are financially constrained beyond survival levels. As a result, we see the intellectual capacity of a child no longer a core attribute towards educational excellence but rather, the socio-economic status of that child in terms of freedom from poverty and HIV pandemic. As a result, the majority of children affected by HIV ultimately miss opportunities and chances of accessing and completing basic education.

2.3.1   Children as Caregivers

When guardians/parents become chronically ill, particularly in poor homes, children come under stress in different ways and this continues for the rest of their childhood. Some take up heavy burdens to nurse chronically ill family members. As a result, they inevitably forgo opportunities to attend school. A survey in Uganda reveals that of children from households affected with HIV, 26% said their attendance at school declined. This was so because of the need to stay at home to take care of their parents, attend to increased household responsibilities and falling household incomes (UNICEF Report, 2003:25).

Bicego, Rutstein and Johnson (2003:6) also suggest that orphaned and other children at risk are less likely to be in school and are more likely to fall behind, drop out and completely lose out on educational prospects. In Zambia, a DHS (1997 -2001) survey reveals the following statistics on the number of orphaned children unlikely to be in schools by 2010 due to HIV impact (CSO, (2001) and (DHS 1997-2001),

- Botswana 94%
- Uganda (88%),
- Equatorial Guinea (84%)

17

- Ghana has (75%) and
- Zambia (68%)

In addition to reduced opportunities to attend school, children become psychologically affected in many ways. For instance, they are too young to shoulder the burden of being breadwinners and also the mere fact that they look after chronically ill persons who have with little hope to survive.

2.3.2 Demographical Impact of HIV Pandemic

The impact of HIV has long-term effect on a country's population growth and stability. In Southern Africa, of which Zambia is part of, the population is projected to reduce by ¼ in 2010 UNICEF Report, 2003:25). The report further suggests that the number of children in secondary schools will reduce by 14% by 2010 due to HIV pandemic.

The aforementioned scenarios bring require coordinated efforts by government and other stakeholders to design support mechanisms that can prevent, reduce and sustain the fight against HIV and AIDS on households and children's access to education.

2.3.3 Impact of Stigma and Discrimination

As a result of loss of parents due to HIV related illness, many children also suffer stigma and discrimination from their peers in schools, homes and communities. Unfortunately, this has an effect on affected children's level of interaction with in class and in recreation events. In most cases, the majority of these children fail to cope with and end up hating school and completely drop out on account of rejection.

Denis Wood suggests that from his research, the concept of orphanhood due to HIV is less accepted as compared to orphanhood caused by natural causes (Save the Children Sweden, 2008). Further, his finding in Western Province reveals that from the discussions with pupils, psychosocial pressures caused by the stigmatisation and discrimination to HIV affected children in schools and communities is often greater than for the child whose parents die from suspected witchcraft.

18

2.3.4 Impact of HIV and AIDS on Teaching Staff

HIV and AIDS also affect transfer of knowledge and other interaction between teachers and the children. On the other hand, the former United Nations (UN), Committee Chairperson on the Rights of a child, Doek, suggests that teachers and other professionals working in education can and should play a critical role in providing children with relevant and appropriate information on HIV pandemic. In this way, they will be contributing to increased awareness and better understanding of this pandemic and prevent further negative attitudes towards victims of the HIV in their areas of professional work (Doek, 2007). Teachers like others are also prone to contracting the virus and this affects their teaching because of chronic illness. Absenteeism of teacher from class and ultimate deaths are some of the short and long term impact of HIV on educational delivery.

In such scenarios, there is limited and even no interaction between HIV and AIDS affected teachers and the children. The reduction in teacher to pupil interaction affects the delivery of knowledge and as a result, children miss out on learning and knowledge. Gwaba, in her research of on children's access to quality education in Zambia, also suggests that the effect and impact of HIV and AIDS on teaching staff reduces children's learning gains due to illness and absenteeism (Save the Children Sweden, 2008).

2.4 MEASURES ADDRESSING HIV IMPACT

In view of the increasing spread and impact of HIV and AIDS pandemic, both the government and other non state organisations have policies and interventions that seek to address negative impact of HIV and AIDS among affected children and households.

In this case, I discuss measures that both the government and other organisations put into place to prevent and reduce the spread of HIV and AIDS and its impact on educational opportunities for children and those households at risk. In this heading, emphasis will be on policies, legislations, conventions on the part of government and the models used by development organisations and other non state actors.

19

2.4.1 GOVERNMENT POLICIES AND INTERVENTIONAL MODELS

As custodian of all human rights the government through MoE has several measures that seek to improve the delivery of educational services to all children including those with special needs as well as those affected by HIV and AIDS pandemic. The literature review shows that MoE has several social protection instruments aimed at increasing opportunities for vulnerable children to access education. These include infrastructure development, bursaries, school health and nutrition programs, Free Basic Education (FBE) and Educational Grants to Community Schools among others.

Specifically, in guiding principle two (2) of EFA (2002), government democratises education by creating an enabling environment and establishing rules and regulations that protect the right of the various partners to fulfil and have a fair participation in educational delivery and development (MoE, 2007).

2.4.1.1   Government Social Protection Measures

The Zambian government carries out social protection instruments to address crosscutting socio-economic issues such as HIV and AIDS, poverty, education, health care and others affecting vulnerable groups of citizens in Zambia. Social protection is a basic human right and a fundamental means for creating social cohesion, thereby ensuring to achieve social peace and inclusion which can prevent and alleviate poverty, HIV and AIDS and other social inadequacies, normally provided by the government (ILO-IPEC 2006: P52).

In this research, the focus will be on measures implemented by government ministries such as Ministry of Youth, Sports and Child Development (MYSCD), Ministry of Education (MoE), Ministry of Community Development and Social Services (MCDSS) and Ministry of Labour and Social Security (MLSS).

2.4.1.2   Public Welfare Assistance Schemes (PWAS) Measures

The government through MCDSS implements (PWAS) to address the vulnerability of households especially those caring for orphaned children and the aged groups of people in society. Through (PWAS), which was re-launched in 2001, MCDSS provides support to the poor

20

and other destitute households in all the 72 districts of Zambia. This is in form of cash and other resources to mitigate impact of inadequacies and chronic vulnerability. PWAS seeks to empower vulnerable groups to fulfil their basic needs such as healthcare, food, educational fees, and shelter.

In the discussion earlier, poverty was pointed out as one of the factors that cause HIV as well as being a resultant of HIV pandemic. According to Denis Wood at least 151,731 orphaned children and the aged benefited in 2006 and this number increased to 125,307 in 2007, representing a % increase of 17.4%. Though this % may seem insignificant, but it has changed the lives of many vulnerable households in meeting costs of essential basics including transport for children to and from schools, food, and shelter and among others.

Therefore, it can be said that the PWA scheme is an effective government instrument that may improve lives of households affected by HIV and AIDS. Through PWAS, children from benefiting households increase their chances to access basic education and other basic social services. Subsequently vulnerable children are equally accorded the opportunities to compete academically with other children from well to do families. Therefore, when properly designed and managed, PWAS may evolve into a good practice and easily adopted by others to effectively reach out many vulnerable households in society.

2.4.1.3   Free Basic Education and School Grants

According to ILO-IPEC (2006:45), education is vital to the development of children and young people in a number of ways. Education equips children with necessary knowledge, competences, and life skills to function in the present and taking up future opportunities. Specifically, for girls and boys affected by HIV and AIDS, education provides the setting and means for reaching them with knowledge and skills to cope with challenges and establish foundation for their future. In Uganda, schools are increasingly setting up Voluntary Counselling and Testing (VCT) services that enable girls and boys who are affected by HIV and AIDS to be aware and subsequently, access friendly health care services more easily (ILO-IPEC, 2006:45).

21

In addition, ILO-IPEC (2006:48) believes that access to quality basic education is a necessary condition for sustained fight against HIV and AIDS among children affected and or infected. Schools also provide safe havens for children withdrawn from HIV and AIDS influenced conditions such as child labour, commercial sexual exploitation, working in quarries and other equally hazardous conditions at the expense of school.

The Zambian government through EFA (2002) introduced free basic Education (FBE) to improve children's access to quality basic education. Statutory school fees and wearing of school uniforms were abolished The abolition of statutory school fees and uniforms was meant to destroy all educational related costs thereby increasing school enrolment and retention rates.

Literature also indicate that government introduced grants to cover for school operational costs such as buying of learning materials, school desks and other consumables such as chalks and paper. Undoubtedly, this measure resulted into increased basic education school enrolments. Denis Wood also reveals that in this area, FBE policy scored major success and led to doubling number of children enrolling into primary schools. On the other hand maintaining the gains has been challenge (Save the Children Sweden, 2008).

Another challenge associated with the FBE policy is that the abolition of school uniforms draws a line between children from poor and those from elite families As opposed to casual wear, uniforms diffuse the status of children because everyone has the same attire. In the end, children from poor families would feel out of place and this is another form of stigmatisation and isolation of vulnerable children in the eyes of the school authorities and fellow children.

Similarly, it is argued that the FBE policy focussed more on mass enrolment than quality output and outcomes. It is argued that very little capacity building and school infrastructure development/improvement, supply of learning materials including the number of teachers to teach the large numbers of classes. Ultimately, the quality of teaching delivered to majority of children is below standards due to factors mentioned above. In addition, grants given to schools are rarely used for improving school learning infrastructure, teaching and reading materials. In

22

most cases, such grants end up on subsidising teacher remunerations, buying of teachers' furniture, which affects the learning delivery and quality of education given to children.

2.4.1.4 Improvement in Infrastructure and Enrolments

The capacity and quality of learning infrastructure affects the number of children each school can take in per calendar year. As at April 2007, Zambia had at least 8,596 high and basic schools and out of these, 8,013 are basic schools and the remaining are high schools (Gwaba, Save the Children, 2008). These include 3,000 new classrooms built between 1999 and 2003 and the 1,600 existing classrooms rehabilitated to date.

There has been an increase in the number of schools offering grades 1-7 from 4,021 in 2006 to 4,269, while those offering grades 1-9 increased from 2,221 to 2,498 during the same period ([1] MoE Educational Bulletin, 2007). However, there was a decline from 246 to 208 and 135 to 95 for 2007 in the number of schools offering grades 1-12 and 10-12 respectively. In addition to learning classroom, government attaches its importance to water and sanitation issues in order to make learning more environmentally friendly. This can be inferred by government's commitment to drill about 1,190 school boreholes in the period 1999 to 2003 (Beyani, 2008).

In his research on advancement of children's rights and the education budget in Zambia, Beyani reveals that policy implementation by government in 1999 to 2003 was acquisition and distribution of desks to schools. However, the number of desks is much fewer than the demand for such desks if one was to compare the pupil to desk ratio, the ratio is not attractive because there too many children against one desk. This is equally the case with the pupil to text book or learning material ratio. As a result, any children still sit on the floor and or benches which make learning and concentration a bit uncomfortable.

2.4.1.5 School Grants and Bursary Schemes

Government introduced school grants in 2002. This scheme provides financial grants to government and other grant aided schools throughout Zambia. Through this strategy, the government seeks to provide all children from grades one to nine free and compulsory basic educations. In addition, MoE manages the bursary scheme that target vulnerable children to

23

access higher and tertiary education. Unlike like the school grants, the bursary scheme specifically targets vulnerable children without financial capacity to met cost of education in high and tertiary levels.

The MoE Educational Bulletin suggests that the impact of School Grants Schemes has also contributed to improvement in enrolment and retention rates in schools. According to MoE and MFNP (2006), the number of grant aided schools increased from 4,622 in 2005 to 4,705 in 2006; access to education rose from 93.5% in 2005 to 95.7% in 2006. On the other hand, the average completion rates for Grade 7 rose from 80.9% in 2005 to 85.5% in 2006 while that of Grade 9 improved from 42.7% in 2006 to 43.1% in 2006.

2.4.1.6   Government Policy to Eliminate Child Labour

Child labour is a product or cause of HIV and AIDS and has significant impact on vulnerable children's access to education. Specifically, the International Labour Organisation (ILO) is working with the government ministry of labour and local development organisations to eliminate Worst Forms of Child Labour. Interventional revolve around addressing ILO Convention 182 on worst forms of child labour and Convention 138 on minimum years of addition to labour market. Many development organisations provide direct educational support services, empowerment initiatives and recreational services. Mainly, four measures are being provided by government and development organisations namely protective, preventive, promotive and transformative. The protective measures are those that protect children from sliding into hazardous situations such as child labour, commercial sex exploitation among others and eventually ending into contracting the HIV virus.

The preventive ones are those measures designed to avert deprivation of services as a result of the existent of influencing factor to HIV and child labour. The promotive measures seek to enhance incomes and capabilities of children and their caregivers to mitigate the impact of HIV and AIDS by avoiding further vulnerability of households and children to involuntarily and voluntarily entering into child labour and subsequently contracting HIV virus respectively. In other words, this measure encourages empowerment of children and caregivers with information and resources for awareness and meeting basic needs respectively.

24

The last measure is the transformative that seeks to challenge the underlying cause of inequalities and social imbalance which includes household division of resource ownership, access and its use. Advocacy against discrimination and stigmatisation of HIV and AIDS affected children in schools is a transformative measure because it seeks to change public perceptions and attitudes on social equity (ILO-IPEC, 2006).

2.4.2   SUSTAINABILITY AND CHALLENGES

2.4.2.1 Government Policies and Sustainability

The commitments by government to HIV and AIDS mitigation and provision of education to children are significant. Through policy formulation, implementation, and monitoring, government has necessary structures that seek to address HIV and AIDS and provision of educational services to children. These policies are likely to be sustainable because they are instruments of government, which is the custodian of legislations including prioritising in budgetary allocation and prudent expenditure.

When government becomes prudent, consistent, and timely in budgetary allocation and management of HIV and AIDS programs, many children are likely to access basic quality education.

2.4.2.2 Limitations

Though Governments recognise that children have the right to education as provided for in the international conventions (UN CRC (1989), ACRWC (2002), MDGs (2000), EFA (2002), they also lack enforcement to compel action. In Zambia, the right to education is not justiciable once denied by government and any other provider as it is not part of the bill of rights in the Zambian constitution. Chanda suggests that though the bill of rights in the Zambian Constitution guarantees every child the right to protection, such constitutional provisions do not go far enough in offering the kind of protection envisaged under the UN CRC (1989). Under the constitution, the provisions do not legally bind, but are directive principles of the state policy, which are not justiciable in the court of law.

Further international instruments such UN CRC, 1989 and others merely make recommendations that state parties ought to follow up but do not have strong monitoring mechanisms apart from the periodic peer review reports presented by government after a period of time

2.5   DEVELOPMENT ORGANISATIONS AND THEIR IMPACT

In this area, I analyse the different models that are used by development organisations and communities to reduce the HIV and AIDS impact on children with special emphasis to those that facilitate children's access to education. Available desk literature reveals that many development organisations carryout HIV and AIDS interventions which are mostly similar in design and implementation. In addition to direct educational and other services, some development organisations also provide both financial and technical support to government through MoE and other relevant ministries.

The United States Agency for International Development (USAID) through CHANGES 2 Project supports MoE Sector Plan. In addition, the project provides bursaries to 7,582 children drawn from 400 government high schools per year for a 5 year period. Similarly, the Times of Zambia reports that a donor from Italy support 517 orphaned and other vulnerable children at Sathya Sai School in Ndola with education requisite to promote girl child education (Times of Zambia, May 13th 2008).

2.5.1   Bursary Scheme and Scholastic Materials Support

Updates and other literature review indicate that many development organisations (both local and international) provide bursaries and other educational support to vulnerable children in basic and or high schools. However, only a few of those interviewed extend their support to tertiary education. By providing bursaries, it is assumed that children are unlikely to drop out of schools including exposure to vulnerable conditions such as engaging into vices that expose them to HIV and AIDS infection.

On the other hand, Project Concern International (PCI) intends to support 144, 749 children with bursary and other direct educational support services for a 5 year period starting from 2007 to 2011. Plan International Zambia, in partnership with USAID has rehabilitated old school

26

classroom structures and constructed new ones including toilets at Mutuvu Basic School in Chibombo District at a total cost of $60,000 (Times of Zambia, May 9, 2008).

2.5.2 Withdraw and Prevention of Children from HIV induced Child Labour

The ILO-IPEC support development organisations to eliminate child labour as a means to reduce further vulnerability of children to the pandemic. They provide direct educational support services as well as indirect support through recreation and empowering the caregivers in communities. The literature from ILO indicates that currently, there are two major projects worthy mentioning in relation to this research

2.5.2.1 ILO-IPEC Child Labour induced HIV Project

The first one is the HIV induced child labour project in implemented in Lusaka, Livingstone, Kapiri Mposhi and Luanshya districts. In this project support, five (5) local development organisations namely CHEP, Zambia Red Cross Society, Jesus Cares Ministries, Tansitha and Livingstone Children's Project are the implementing agencies. They provide educational support services to children whose households are directly and indirectly affected by HIV and AIDS. In addition, they provide business enterprise empowerment to care givers to sustain the support once the three (3) year support ends in 2009.

The literature established that three categories of beneficiaries affected by HIV are targeted. The first group of vulnerable children are those already dropped out of schools as a result of HIV and AIDS related factors and are already engaged in child labour. These children are withdrawn from such hazardous environments and reintegrated back into the conventional and community schools. However, a few of those children especially those beyond basic education, are supported with vocational skills training and provided with start up kits to start their businesses once they complete training.

The second category involves children affected by the HIV and AIDS and other related factors still in schools but there are high possibilities that they will also drop out of schools. This category of children is also provided with direct school requisites to remain in schools.

27

The third category includes the caregivers. These benefit in form of household empowerment with business enterprise support. The idea behind is to build the financial foundation to sustain the children prevented and those withdrawn and reintegrated back into convention and community schools. As said earlier, this project has a maximum of three years and after this, ILO will no long provide funding to meet the school requisites for the children currently supported, hence the need to develop sustainability measures.

Table 2.5.2.1 shows a summary of target number of children affected by HIV prevented from dropping out of schools as well as those withdrawn from worst forms of child labour due to HIV and poverty vulnerability. It also shows the target number of care- givers meant for empowerment as a long term sustainability mechanism for children currently supported. All the strategic interventions also indicate the progress made wards achieving the set targets as at September 2008 peer review evaluation.

Table 2.5.2.1

	Non state actor	Target Number		Progress Made	
		Prevention	Withdraw	Prevention	Withdraw
1	Jesus Cares Ministries	270	250	253	290
2	Tasintha	243	200	192	163
3	CHEP	200	200	131	263
4	LAC Project	200	200	200	166
5	Zambia Red Cross	160	140	197	134
Total		1073	990	973	1,016

Notes: (i) **Prevented** means children affected by HIV but are still in schools that require support to avoid sliding into child labour or dropping out of school

(ii) **Withdrawn** means children who already dropped out of school due to impact of HIV and poverty individually or collectively and working in dangerous environments where they are taken and reintegrated back into educational system

2.5.2.2 ILO-IPEC Time Bound Program on Child Labour

The second intervention on HIV and AIDS by the ILO-IPEC, Zambia is the Time Bound Project on elimination of child labour. Through this, children infected and affected by HIV and AIDS and those at risk of dropping out school due to vulnerability to poverty and HIV and AIDS are prevented while those in hazardous conditions are withdrawn and reintegrated back into conventional and community schools. Care-givers are also given empowerment opportunities in business enterprises. In addition, the project provides recreational opportunities for children at risk and those already affected by HIV and AIDS including child labour.

In this project support, eight (8) local agencies namely Jesus Cares Ministries, Community Youth Concern, Hosanna Mapalo, Children In Crisis, Zambia Federation of Employers, Zambia Congress of Trade Unions, ANPPCAN Zambia including Ministry of Education through the Zambia Institute of Special Education (ZAMISE) and the Ministry of Labour. The intervention benefits children, policy makers and communities in Lusaka, Central Copperbelt, Northern and Luapula Provinces.

As in the HIV and AIDS induced child labour project discussed earlier, the ILO-IPEC supported Time Bound Project also uses four measures to address and prevent vulnerability of children to inadequacies in form of protective, preventive, promotive and transformative measures. This shows realisation by key players on the magnitude and impact of HIV and its direct and indirect relationship with poverty, child labour and other causal and effect factors. This also shows how stakeholders appreciate synergy of coordinated efforts if the fight against HIV and AIDS, poverty and child labour were to be won. Ultimately, the rights of children can be realised and upheld in society.

Table 2.5.2.2 shows a summary of progress made in achieving the milestone of the TBP support project with regards to eliminating child labour, reducing HIV and poverty vulnerability among children and households of their caregivers. It also shows the government progress in policy formulation through formation of District Child Labour Committees (DCLCs) as well as establishing the Community Child Labour Committees (CCLCs) in order to monitor and provide surveillance on current and potential cases of child labour induced HIV pandemic.

It should be noted that the % progress was as at the mid way of the project. And also the lower rates of achievements on business enterprise support by a number of partners already replicating the models require adequate time for implementation. Table 2.5.2.2 shows progress made and indicators scored by non state actors according different sources of desk literature.

Table 2.5.2.2

No	Indicator	Indicator target details		
		Target	Actual	%
1	No of children affected and or at risk of affected by HIV and child labour supported with educational requisites	10,000	6,842	86.42
2	No of care givers empowered with IGAs	4,000	400	10
3	No. of organisations providing direct services to children	8	8	100
4	No. of organisations expressing interest in replicating the models of interventions	25	5	20
5	No. of children empowered with recreation facilities to reduce their vulnerability to HIV and child labour	5,000	2,000	40
6	No of recreational facilities created	8	3	37.5
Total		19,041	9,258	

2.5.3 Comparative Data about Stakeholders in other Countries

There are similarities in design and implementations of HIV and AIDS programs and service delivery across the globe. In Namibia, Catholic AIDS Action (CAA) paid school fees and bought uniforms and procured scholastic materials for 950 children in conventional schools to cover educational costs for 3 years (Firelight Foundation Report, 2003). The concern therefore is the fate of the 950 children with regards to uniforms, schools fees and scholastic materials after 3 years. What happens to 950 children if no sustainable measures were put in place especially that uniforms are a cardinal requirement for children?

Lyambo also acknowledges the importance of uniforms in motivating children and how this critical component drives children to attending school. Unfortunately, children without school uniforms may face discrimination such as having them sit on the floor with gloomy faces, while their counterparts in uniforms walk heads high, carry big smiles on their faces, feel proud and happy, and sit in front of the classroom. *One 15 year old pupil had this to say, 'Our school is different from other schools because we are given lunch, clothes, shoes and pens. We are also treated for free when we fall sick' (Firelight Annual Report 2003:29).* Hence, such support requires sustainability for both current and scaling up support.

2.5.4 Support to School Infrastructural Development

In addition to technical support to MoE, CHANGES 2 seeks to improve vulnerable children's access to education through grants to improve learning infrastructure, which is done in partnership with communities. Through grants, community schools including some government schools are able to improve learning environments in terms of capacity, security from sun and rains in schools where children learn under trees, in grass thatched building and among others. According to CHANGES 2, community partnership is a good practice that must be cultivated because it forms the basis for effective intervention, integration and sustainability with local communities.

The Japanese Ambassador to Zambia, Mr. Hideto Mitamura also values the importance of local people taking charge of donor supported projects to ensure continuity after donors have pulled out (Chanda, (2008), Times of Zambia). Children In Crisis (CIC) also agrees with the ambassador's views because giving handouts alone is not sustainable but where handouts are given should be accompanied by household and community empowerment support to build long term capacity. CIC suggests that social protection measures such as business ventures appropriate to the need and capacity of the beneficiary groups must be given (Children In Crisis, Bulletin (2007).

In a bid to improve community school operations CHANGES 2 Project has set aside a small grants budget to support sixty seven (67) community schools in infrastructure development for a five (5) year period (CHAGNES 2, 2005 to 2009).

31

2.5.5   Training and Capacity Building Initiatives

A CHANGE 2 supports MoE to strengthen teachers' basic education and professional skills in order to reduce the vulnerability of teachers and children to HIV and AIDS pandemic. The training aims at empowering teachers, pupils and community members with knowledge and skills in order to improve provision and access to education, gender equity, promoting health standards in schools including HIV prevention.

ILO – IPEC (2006:49), is of the view that the fight against stigma and discrimination on children affected and infected by IIIV and AIDS in schools can only succeed when teachers and other community members are trained in HIV and AIDS skills to offer counselling and other psychosocial support. ILO-IPEC further indicates that todate, even when there is overwhelming scientific evidence that HIV cannot be spread through means such as touch and or sharing utensils, negative attitudes still exist. Unfortunately, this result into isolation and rejection of affected and infected children and ultimately drops out of school (ILO-IPEC, 2006).

In this strategy, about 800 teachers from government basic schools has been targeted for skills training in HIV and AIDS per year which means for a five year period, about 4,000 teacher will have acquired life skills in HIV and IIDS prevention. On the other hand, Project Concern International (PCI) is providing capacity building training to forty nine (49) community school teachers in school management and lesson planning. In addition, the organisation also provides training in management skills to forty nine (49) Parent Teachers' Association (PTA) committees (PCI, Bulletin. 2006:2). CHANGES 2 notes that training of teachers and PTA committees is a good practice that can enhance the rate at which communities can actively participate in educational service delivery and management.

When communities take centre stage in educational service management, it is likely that they would effectively mobilise themselves to develop learning infrastructure and collectively address any matter that affect children's access to education in their communities.

2.5.6 Provision of Text Books and other Learning Materials

Development organisations participate in provision of learning materials such as textbooks, teachers' reference guides to community and government schools. Some literature review indicates that development organisations really fill the gap in provision of learning materials to schools. Without their support, the teacher to pupil and pupil to textbook ratios could have been extremely undesirable. However, with their support many schools and children have benefited from teaching and other learning materials including the enhancement of enrolment and retention rates.

The literature review suggests that development organisations participation in educational service delivery goes beyond individual vulnerable children. Construction of school infrastructure and desks alone is not an end, but also providing learning materials and capital infrastructures. The available literature indicates that after USAID and Plan Zambia constructed and rehabilitated school infrastructure at Mutuvu Basic School in Chibombo they also provided 160 textbooks and 80 desks.

According to estimates, the new school facelift will see an increase in the enrolment rates from 420 to 600 children, representing a 45% increment. Plan International Zambia is optimistic that good results are expected from this school because infrastructural and other environmental problems that children, parents, and teachers faced since 1982 are long gone (Times of Zambia May 9, 2008).

2.5.7 Economic Empowerment of Caregivers

The literature also reveals that one of the models used to address long-term impact of HIV and AIDS is empowerment of caregivers. Mostly, empowerment is through provision of management skills and knowledge. ILO describe empowerment as a way of giving someone information, skills and capacity to do what is required in order to respond to a given situation meaningfully. This includes training children in HIV and child labour life skills in order to effectively, reason, decide and solve and or prevent problems arising from HIV and child labour (2006: P42). Secondly empowerment also means provision of resources and donations for direct consumption to enables recipients generate their own resources thereafter. This is done by supporting poultry projects to generate income for buying scholastic materials upon completion of external support.

2.6.   LIMITATIONS AND CHALLENGES OF EMPOWERMENT

2.6.1   Inadequate Start up Capital

In this competitive economy, the magnitude of capital for business enterprise must be adequate to meet high costs of inputs, payment towards costs of production, labour and transportation of both inputs and outputs. As a result, business enterprises pose a challenge due to aforementioned factors. Some empowerment models end at imparting and acquisition of skills and knowledge and do not provide start up capital. This makes it rather difficult to implement practical empowerment. As a result, children are unlikely to continue in school due to lack of the envisaged income for long term educational costs.

2.6.2   Diversion of Capital to other Essentials

The target groups for empowerment are vulnerable households without any form of capital to meet their basic needs such as food, shelter, and clothing. Such households are likely to divert the little capital to buy basic essentials such as food, medical school and others.

2.6.3 High Competition in the Market

In market a driven economy, competition, is high. Unfortunately, small vendors are subjected to stiff competition by bigger competitors whose businesses enjoy economies of scale and existing good will with customers. Start up capital is usually too small to produce the kind of products that can compete effectively with bigger competitors.

2.6.4   Similarities of Empowerment Models

The business enterprise must provide goods and services meeting potential demand in a market. It is important that vendors produce goods and services that meet and satisfy a unique and identifiable niche in the market. Unfortunately, what is seen is that most of the empowerment business activities are very similar and revolve within carpentry, tailoring, selling fruiters and scorns, selling of second hand clothes among others. It is common to find hundreds of similar business enterprise within one market place targeting the same and limited consumers. As a result, there are more sellers of similar products and services than buyers. This does not work well to the seller because buyers will have strong negotiation powers (buyer's market).

This could be attributed to lack of market research. As a result, business enterprise promoters leave out high demand niche without being identified and hence not explored for investments. I feel that that business empowerment must be demand driven rather than being donor driven. In addition, I goods and services must be innovative so that they are dynamic and responsive to appeal to needs and expectation of the potential demand in the market.

2.7   LIMITATIONS AND CHALLENGES FACED

The dependence on external funding has major limitations on timely resource allocation and expending. This also affects the sustainability of activities especially that they are usually for shorter timeframes. In addition, non-state actors or development organisations do not generate their own resources to timely meet educational needs of affected target groups. Further, external support is always time bound and upon completion of agreed output and duration, such support end. It can also shift to other needy beneficiaries even though the problems with current target groups have not been conclusively addressed. As a result, many projects end without holistically addressing the problems.

2.8   COMMUNITY SCHOOL EDUCATION IN ZAMBIA

Communities and Community Schools are cardinal partners in education service provision including mitigation of HIV and AIDS in Zambia. According to MoE Strategic Framework, community schools appeared in the country in 1992, beginning with Lusaka and quickly spread to other parts of Zambia due to socio-economic factors (MoE, 2007). In 1996, there were only 95 Community Schools in the country and this figure rose for more than 50 times reaching 2,477 officially known community schools as at 2007.

2.8.1   Impact and Sustainability

Community schools like non state actors or development organisations address gaps left by conventional education delivery mechanisms due geographical and other factors. According to MoE, community schools have progressively catered for high number of orphans in terms of access to education (MoE- EMIS, 2007).`Further, MoE literature shows that there are 48.5% orphans in community schools as compared to 46.8% in government schools as at 2006. This indicates that community schools play a critical role providing accessibility (MoE Strategic Framework for Community Schools (2007-2010).

Under the coordination of Zambia Community Schools Secretariat (ZCSS) then, community schools follow national education curriculum. Community schools which meet MoE standards become examination centres like other government schools. They conduct Grade 7 examinations and candidates equally compete for Grade 8 places with their counterparts from conventional schools.

From the national assessment of learning achievements conducted in 2003 in community schools, statistics show that learning is taking place in community schools and quality education is being offered by many of them. This is in spite of difficult circumstances (lack of environmentally friendly learning infrastructure, lack of teaching materials and qualified teachers, impoverished communities and among other factors).

However, community schools can only reach and meet MoE standards when community members are committed and raise resources for school infrastructures and payment of community school volunteers. In Malawi for instance, Community-based Options for the Protection and Empowerment (COPE) local development organisation funded by Save the Children, USA, has demonstrated a systematic approach to mobilising community-based resources. The resources raised support orphaned and those at risk in the communities. Similarly, in Tanzania, villagers set up 'Most Vulnerable Committees' (MVCs) that mobilise and distribute donations from local well wishers and also organise business ventures and to promote the rights and welfare of children in the community (Donahue and Williamson, 1999).

In Swaziland, local people set up committees to pool resources together for organised community support towards education of vulnerable children in their communities. One committee successfully set up a shop at a local basic school whose income pays school fees to sustain several vulnerable children.

36

2.8.2 Capacity Building Teaching Staff

Many heads of community schools lack teaching and school management skills. This affects coordination and management of human, financial, and other community school materials and resources. Literature from CHANGES 2 indicates that lack of management skills ultimately affects the quality of education given to children. To address this gap, the CHANGES 2 provides management training targeting at least five hundred (500) community school head teachers.

In addition, another five hundred (500) ordinary community school teachers are being trained in basic teaching skills, lesson planning, classroom management and community partnership management. In addition, the project provides textbooks to 500 community schools. This has improved teachers' teaching delivery kills and class management in the beneficiary community schools. Ultimately, there is an improvement in the quality of education given to children in community schools whose teachers have been trained.

2.8.3 Monitoring and Quality Assurance of Standards

In order to monitor the quality of education delivered in community schools, CHANGES 2 as trained thirty (30) District and Provincial level MoE staff to monitor, supervise and provide technical support to community schools (CHANGES 2, 2005-2009).

2.8.4 Challenges of Community School Education Delivery

The challenges of delivery in community schools include lack of learning infrastructure. Children learn in dilapidated structures and at times, in open spaces such as under trees, unfinished buildings, grass thatched classes and others.

Secondly, most of the teachers manning and teaching in community schools are not qualified and experienced teachers. Mostly, they have only attended short and tailored courses. A few qualified teachers only go to community schools when waiting for government postings. Immediately they are given postings, they leave for government teaching positions.

Thirdly, community schools lack adequate teaching and learning materials such as textbooks for children and reference books for teachers. This, too, affects teaching delivery and children's own reading and understanding.

2.9 IMPACT OF PRIVATE SECTOR INTERVENTIONS

The private sector is another partner that contributes towards children's access to education including HIV and AIDS mitigation. Apart from corporate social responsibility, the private sector plays a major role towards reducing impact of HIV and AIDS through HIV and AIDS work place policies. In addition, the private sector directly and indirectly contributes to educational delivery through private schools and also donation to government and community schools.

Konkola Copper Mines (KCM) has set aside five hundred thousand US Dollars ($500,000) equivalent of ZMK1.7 billion under its corporate social responsibility. This money is meant to assist government schools in Chililabombwe, Chingola, Kitwe and Nampundwe Districts with equipment and support for learning (Phiri, 2008). About 300 and 19 computers and printers respectively are being installed in schools, too. In addition, 21 information technology staff has also been employed to provide maintenance services for a period of 5 years.

The aforementioned is evident inclusive involvement of stakeholders if provisional and delivery of quality education was to be meaningfully done. After all, the outcome is beneficial to individuals and national socio-economic development. KCM believes that quality computer skills are vital in the knowledge-based global economy and therefore the need to prepare the children with appropriate educational skills and knowledge for meaningful contribution in the scientific and technological sector.

2.10 GOOD PRACTICES AND SUSTAINABILITY

From literature review, I indicate some of the good practices that contribute towards reducing of impact of HIV and AIDS in Zambia and ultimately, promotion of children's access to basic education. Good practices may not be stand alone but a combination of interventions.

2.10.1 Government Policy on Inclusive Participation

Government policy on inclusive participation in education delivery can be cited as a good practice. The policy attracts capital investment in infrastructure development and other areas of educational service delivery in Zambian. In addition, by inclusive participation, the HIV and AIDS pandemic can easily be addressed through combined forces varying from policy, financial and technical expertise of different stakeholders.

In addition, inclusive participation can enhance capacity of teachers and PTA committees especially those from community schools. Expertise from corporate sector and civil society organizations are cardinal in the fight against HIV and AIDS pandemic. The corporate sector has money to sustain their interventions while non state actors' competitive edge revolves around their ability to target and their specific expertise and niches.

2.10.2 Community Partnership in School Management

The involvement of communities in school management, through partnership, is a good practice that can enhance and sustain vulnerable children's access to basic education. Its competitive edge is the ability to build capacity of the communities to continue managing the interventions after the phase out of external support. Swanpoel also suggests that a sustainable intervention is one that builds the capacity of local people so that they plan, implement, monitor and manage outcomes and outputs without external technical and resource inputs (Swanpoel, 1998).

2.11 SUMMARY AND CONCLUSION OF CHAPTER

2.11.1 Government

Government as duty bearer provide a policy mechanism towards HIV and AIDS mitigation by creating HIV and AIDS coordinating body, namely National AIDS Council. It has also mainstreamed HIV and AIDS through multi-sectoral response mechanisms. In terms of educational policies, the Educational Policy (1996), EFA (1990 & 2002), and MDGs (2000) are some of government policies that facilitate education delivery. However, there is still a lot that government needs to do if the right to education was to be a reality. Education accessibility still has many hidden costs such as PTA fees, which have replaced statutory school fees deemed to have been abolished in 2002.

Further, signing and ratification of the UN CRC (1989) and the ACRWC (2002) are some of the international conventions that show government's commitment to promotion of the rights of children. However, government still needs to do more especially in domesticating some and if all provisions of the aforementioned international conventions. In the current constitution, the right to education falls in the directive principles of the state and as such, this right cannot be justiciable in the court of law once denied.

Further, there is increasing commitment from government to respond to the needs of vulnerable children. This is evidenced by increased budgetary allocation to children's activities and programs However, there seems to be a lot of duplication of activities and policies among the various ministries.

2.11.2 The Non State Actors and Communities

These have contributed towards addressing needs of vulnerable children through HIV and AIDS mitigation in general and children's access to basic education. Various models are being used to meet the needs of children, schools and the government stakeholders. However, most of the activities depend on external support, which affects sustainability.

CHAPTER 3

3.0 RESEARCH METHODOLOGY

3.1 INTRODUCTION

This chapter attempts to explore various research techniques and the methodology that were used to gather both primary and secondary data of the study. This study is more of explorative as is attempts to provide answers as to whether HIV and AIDS affect children's educational opportunities. Secondly, the study attempts to outline the relevance and effectiveness of education models in mitigating impact of HIV pandemic. The study also attempts to assess relevance and applicability of government policies and international conventions and responses to mitigate impact of HIV on education.

Thirdly, the study seeks to explore and analyse the limitations and ability of policies, and international conventions towards addressing HIV and AIDS on education accessibility. In the same line, the research also seeks to explore and analyse the limitations and sustainability of models in responding to HIV pandemic and education service provision.

3.2 RATIONALE OF THE STUDY

This research study is comprehensive and encompassing in design and execution. In total, it involved five different key respondents deemed key in the study. Questionnaires and where necessary, personal interviews were used to collect primary data while desk review was used to collect secondary data. It is important to assess the negative impact of HIV and AIDS on children and its subsequent effect on educational opportunities. Specifically, it is important to evaluate the impact of support given to educating children affected by HIV and AIDS. The research also provides an opportunity to development practitioners, donors and government to assess the effectiveness of HIV and AIDS mitigation among children.

In addition, the research analyses the gaps and opportunities that different key players encounter and to high light some of those that can be further explored. The research looks at sustainability of strategies and approaches in the fight against HIV and AIDS and access to education. This research will also provide a base for stakeholders to design interventional initiatives. As Parcel points out, evidence - based qualitative research methods can generate new and valid data and findings needed for effective decision-making in development programming (Parcel etal 2005).

Donors are increasingly developing aid fatigue, which is coupled with changes in their development aid policies. Many development oriented stakeholders especially those that use external funding may appreciate importance of this research. It will be an eye opener especially those depending on external resources and have no intention of exploring sustainable sources and means to counteract the decreasing basket of donor support.

Equally, external funding agencies are increasingly faced with financial constraints and this has direct negative impact on the magnitude of support they provide to competing development organisations. Voorhoeve agrees that donors are now faced financial challenges concerning mobilising funds to meet the development needs (WPF Report 2005).

On the other hand, Zambia signed a Memorandum of Understanding (MoU) on 8th April 2005 with major cooperating partners, which among others, provides for donor coordinated aid approach. The implication is that major donors put money into government treasury giving the latter an opportunity to reallocate funds according to key areas of the economy (Milima, 2007).

With this new development approach, the trend is that many development agents no longer receive adequate funding to support educational and other development activities, projects and programs. This research provides information to development agents about importance of designing sustainable activities, projects and programs in view of the financial implication of this change in aid policy by the majority of donors.

External support has specific time limit after which, donors expect results for consideration of possible continuation with same target groups or different ones in the same geographical or different locations respectively. It is important that development organisations and other stakeholders design sustainable projects so that once external support ends, they continue without need for external resources.

Lastly, this research adds to existing body of academic knowledge on impact of HIV on children and how policy and non state actor response mechanism play preventive and remedial roles. It also suggests how education can be a cardinal model in reducing impact of HIV among affected children and households. In addition, the research underscores importance of inclusion of sustainability in intervention to sustain and reduce continued dependency on external resources.

3.3   RESEARCH METHODOLOGY

This research was designed and conducted in a comprehensive and encompassing manner. It involved five (5) different categories of respondents who play particular roles in the problem of study as policy makers, development facilitators, managers and administrators as well as beneficiaries. Both existing literature review and field data was collected to gather data for this study.

In addition, inductive and deductive reasoning techniques were applied when analyzing, presenting, discussing and making conclusion and recommendations. This methodological approach provided representative data for the making conclusion of study findings.

3.4   RESEARCH DESIGN

In carrying out this research, a logical and systematic process was followed. This gave a clear road map and direction. I was able to take stock of pace and progress at each stage of research activity. Each activity was given a time schedule, time frame, resources and materials required including when to do it and who was responsible for execution. This is so because the research involved participation of different respondents.

The starting point was choosing a research problem after taking into account to the extent and magnitude of the problem and also anticipated benefits of the research to the stakeholders. After reflection on a number of topics, a decision was made to carryout a research on impact of HIV and AIDS on Children's education in 4 selected communities in Lusaka district. The reasoning to settle for this topic among others was the growing number of non state actors providing education services to children affected and infected by HIV and AIDS. On the other hand, the HIV pandemic according to literature keeps on increasing. There danger for many actors to

43

abandon children before completing basic education due to pull out of external support on account of continuous dependence on external. Hence, there was need to assess impact, long-term sustainability including taking stock of available strategic practices that have since been developed to effectively reduce HIV and AIDS impact among children.

The choice of research topic was followed by the development of a research proposal that sought to gather data for inference. This was followed by a development of data collection instruments, namely questionnaires and interviews guides. Before administering to final respondents, the questionnaire was pre-tested and a few changes were readjusted.

The above set ground for development of the entire research budget to cater for logistics, paper, telephone, postage, ink for printing and binding of the final copies of the thesis. The next stage was printing and then distribution of questionnaires to sampled respondents which involved deliver and collect later and postage. This was followed by collection of filled questionnaires and conducting personal interviews especially where clarifications were necessary. Personal interview were done on face to face and telephone in some instances. Distribution and collection of filed questionnaires was done in 25 working days instead of the planned 15 working days. This was attributed to bureaucracies and losing of questionnaires especially by some respondents .These stages finally led to sorting, coding, writing of research reports (presentation and analysis of the findings, research conclusion and recommendations).

3.5   SAMPLE SIZE

The total sample was fifty two (**52**) respondents broken down as follows:
- (i)   **10** respondents from development organisations that provide education services to mitigate the HIV and AIDS impact on orphans and other children at risk.
- (ii)   **04** respondents from donor agencies supporting development organisations working in protection and promotion the rights of orphans children and those children at risk
- (iii) **10** respondents from school management where beneficiary children learn
- (iv)   **24** children respondents who are beneficiaries of education support from development organisations still in non tertiary education (grade 1 to 12)

(v)   **04** respondents from the Government line ministries (MCDSS, MYSCD, MoE and Labour)

3.6   SAMPLING METHODOLOGY

The sampling technique employed in this research was purposively because there was need to target responses from respondents falling in the category predetermined. The first stage of sampling was reviewing a list of development organisations and donors from a directly of organisations providing different services to children. This directory was obtained from the mother body of child rights organisations in Zambia, namely Children In Need Network (CHIN). From the same directory, some donors providing resources to development organisations for HIV and AIDS mitigation as well as education were identified and 4 were chosen as part of the research sample.

A sample of ten (10) development organisations was randomly selected. After this, visits were made to selected organisations for administration of questionnaires and personal interview where applicable to serve two (2) purposes namely, selection of geographical locations to conduct the research and schools where supported children learn. After this, 4 communities felt to have representative number of schools from which primary data was children and school managers would be gotten were chosen.

3.7   SCOPE OF THE STUDY

The study was limited to respondents from donors, relevant government ministries and development organisations from within Lusaka. The other two categories of respondents namely school managers and children as beneficiaries were selected from a target of 10 schools from 4 communities in Lusaka, namely Chunga, Matero, Chaisa and George.

3.8   RESEARCH INSTRUMENTS

The research must not restrictive to a single method of data collection (Best and Khan 2003). Various methods and techniques were used to obtain data from the target respondents. They included structured questionnaires, personal interviews and analysing project implementation documents from development organisations and donors. They also reports, and presentations,

45

articles and update briefs. In principle, the methods were employed in order to get a deeper understanding of the research problem which, I quote "The Impact of HIV and AIDS on Education: A case study of 4 communities in Lusaka District, Zambia."

3.8.1 Secondary Data

The secondary data on relationships between HIV and access to education was available. Various reports and publications provided vital literature for study problem. In some cases, the Project Implementation Documents and training manuals provided useful targets and other figures for comparisons and analysis.

In addition, literature on HIV impact on education was also obtained from other countries in Africa. Namibia, Kenya, Uganda and Malawi are some of comparative countries that provided statistical data. The GRZ documents provided government policy positions on HIV and education.

Local newspapers also provided up to date data. Here, the two local dailies, the Post Newspaper and Times of Zambia gave relevant update literature for this research problem.

Another source of secondary data was from research disseminations by consultants on HIV and educational related research problems. In particular, dissemination of findings of different commissioned research among them consultants Gwaba, Wood and Beyani gave vital data on this study.

3.8.2 Primary Data

Primary data of study was collected through personal interviews and structured questionnaires administered to target respondents. The category of respondents involving school managers and beneficiary children in schools were reached through questionnaires posted while others were delivered by development organisations staff to school where they support children.

Data from development organisations was collected through structured questionnaires and personal interviews though most of the questionnaires were answered in the absence of the

46

researcher. Hence the majority questionnaires were left and collected later. This was similar in most of the organisations. There seem to be similar organisational policies that restrict movement of information to external users unless thorough clearance is done by an authorised officer. This is a major limitation because many controlling officers did not authorise their subordinates to answer questionnaires. However, clarifications for a few questionnaires that were not clear were made to validate the data upon collection.

The second sources of primary data were 4 government line ministries (MSYCD, MoE, MLSS and MCDSS). Lastly, attempts were made to get data from donor agencies. A total number of twenty five (25) days were spent to distribute and collect back the questionnaires. Validation and analysis of the findings began with coding of the responses. This was done to remove any response and data component that could have led to inclusion of invalid data in the findings.

A summary of questionnaires delivered and those that were returned, which are the basis of the findings. A combined average of 73% response was attained as indicated in table 3.5.2 below.
Table 3.5.2

No	Respondent	Category	Target	Returned	Rate
1	Children	Beneficiaries	24	22	90%
2	School managers	Schools	10	06	60%
3	Development organisations	Service providers	10	07	70%
4	Donors	Funding agencies	04	02	50%
5	Government	Policy	04	02	50%
6	Total		52	37	73%

3.9   ETHICAL CONSIDERATION

In this study ethical consideration were observed to avoid personal, professional and any other ethical conducts that inflict the interest of respondents, the researcher, institutions or groups of people. Thorough consent to participate in the research was reached at after explanation was given to each respondent before answering the questionnaire. Only those that were agreeable to participate were given questionnaires while those who did not agree, their decision was equally respected.

3.10 BIAS AND LIMITATIONS

This research was designed in such a way that significant bias was minimised. At design stage, key stakeholders were identified so that any biasness could be addressed by cross-checking of data and other information obtained from secondary and primary sources. Different questions were carefully formulated to capture information from five (5) different respondents. At the end of the day, any response that was suspected unrealistic was cross-checked and inferred against the responses from other categories of stakeholders. The analysis was based on 37 out of 52 target respondents who answered and returned the questionnaires.

3.11 DATA ANALYSIS

Data was analysed after sorting and coding of the responses. Sorting was done to remove any inconsistence that could influence wrong outcome of the research. Coding of responses was done in order to group responses and any related data according to the research questions. Once these two processes were thoroughly done, analysis of the findings was done. Four (4) major tools, namely, percentages (%), pie charts, graphs and cross tabulation to supplement the discussions in the presentation and analysis were used.

3.12 SUMMARY OF THE CHAPTER

As stated already in the introduction, the study was more of explorative in order infer as to whether HIV and AIDS have an impact on children and their educational opportunities in 4 selected communities. It also sought to provide answers as to whether government and development organisations practical respond to impact of HIV pandemic. And if so, how sustainable are those approaches and models in responding to impact?

The research methodologies used included personal interviews and administering of questionnaires to selected respondents. In addition, secondary data was collected from reports in other countries within Africa. This made this research comparative because statistics from comparator countries was vital. Therefore, the analysis is broad minded. The data was further classified into secondary and primary data with secondary data being data obtained from existing literatures. Primary data comprised of data obtained through interviews and administered questionnaires specifically meant for this research.

CHAPTER 4

4.0   PRESENTATION OF RESEARCH FINDINGS

4.1   INTRODUCTION

In this chapter, the findings of the study are presented based on responses from questionnaires administered to respondents, personal interviews and also review of desk literature. The desk research was obtained from books and other publications, researchers and scholars, government policy documents, international human rights conventions, donor and development organizations reports within Zambia and other African countries. The findings presented in this chapter seek and attempt to provide answers to the research problems.

4.2   FORMAT OF THE QUESTIONNAIRE

Five (5) categories of questionnaires were designed for different types of respondents. Each type had specific questions that suit the data, which was being sought. They are attached as appendices **No. 4.2.1-5**

4.3   THE HIV PREVALENCE AND IMPACT

HIV and AIDS affect the socio-economic productivity and subsequent availability of essential basics in the market. In turn, this affects individual households and children who are left as orphans upon death of parents and other close members of extended families. It is argued that HIV and AIDS mostly affect people in prime age groups and thereby, producing orphaned children in tender ages without capacity to safely take care of themselves (http://web.worldbank.org).

4.4   RELATIONSHIP BETWEEN HIV AND EDUCATION

Various literature show close linkages between HIV and AIDS and its effect on children's access to education. Such linkages are in a number of ways. For instance, the death of parents and other breadwinners affect household incomes, care and provision of essential services including education. This effect can be felt in terms of lack of education requisites such as school fees, transport money to and from school, adequate household food security among others.

49

Though education is being regarded as free in Zambia, there are quite a number of hidden costs that hinder children from poor households to access educational opportunities. In addition, HIV and AIDS is a chronic illness that has an impact on people's contribution to socio-economic productivity. Literature indicates that quite substantial amount of man hours are lost through nursing chronic ill members of families. In addition, a lot of productive time is also spent on attending to burials of those dying of the pandemic.

4.5   REDUCING OF HIV IMPACT ON CHILDREN'S EDUCATION

In this part, I present the findings of the research from primary sources. The findings are divided into five (5) parts.

4.5.1   Findings from Development Organizations

Of the eight (8) questionnaires successfully filled and returned by this category of respondents, all respondents indicated that HIV and AIDS was a factor in their programming. They also mentioned that education was one of the strategies that they use to reduce impact of HIV among target children and households in communities. The respondents also indicate the existence of close relationship between poverty and HIV and AIDS. Poverty and HIV either individually or collectively have negative impact on delivery and accessibility of education by children. According to them, deaths of parents/guardians or chronic illness of parents affect on their productivity, income and access to basic essentials

In terms of magnitude of HIV and AIDS impact on gender parity, five (5) out of eight (8) respondents indicated that girls are more vulnerable to the pandemic than boys. This represents girl to boy vulnerability and infection ratio of 63.5% to 36.5%, almost 2:1. Interestingly, poverty was linked to spread and impact of HIV by all respondents, including those who said the pandemic affected boys and girls equally. In their argument, girls' vulnerability is due to survival and coping mechanism which include commercial sex exploitation to raise money and other materials needs for household consumption. In Nigeria, Dr. Chika also explains that many children orphaned by the HIV and AIDS engage in blacksmithing, trapping and hunting, trading and schooling is the least priority.

50

In terms of target, all the respondents provide educational support to both girls and boys within the age group of 0 to 18 years as provided for by UN CRC (1989). However they differ on the age to starting supporting them with education. Of the 8 respondents, only 37.5% start their support right early childhood education while 62.5% start from grade one. Fifty (50%) of respondents extend their educational support to tertiary education including vocational skills training while the other 50% end at basic and high school. With regards to driving passion, all the respondents indicated children from age 0 to 18 are highly vulnerable because their safety and care depend on goodwill of adults (parents and guardians, teachers, career givers and communities they live).

Respondents view education as a backbone for a solid foundation to a solid socio-economic growth and security. They envisage that provision of education to children builds and empower children to participate in productive sectors of the economy. In terms of strategies, 75% respondents provide support using three (3) education models namely, infrastructure development, paying school fees and building capacity of teachers. In addition, 37.5% respondents also provide recreational and food supplements to children.

On sustainability, 7 out of 8 respondents are of the view that development organizations must venture into business to sustain children they support and others equally in need of support. This represents 87.5% in favour of business ventures and 12.5% against. This is illustrated in the pie chart

Table 4.5.1.1

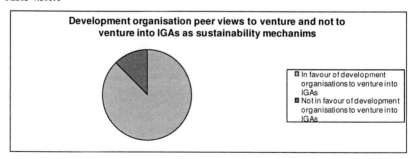

It is argued that business enterprise may reduce total depend on donor resources for interventions and this account for 87.5% of respondents. Donor funded projects have specific timeframes and usually have short project times. Business enterprises can generate a pull of funds from which support to children can be sustained upon project phase out or closure.

On the other hand, the 12.5% were of the view that once development organisations begin venturing into business, they risk lose their original passion for disadvantaged people and become pure capitalist. In terms of available strategic and operational practices, 62.5% identified business enterprises as their main good practices. These range from entrepreneurship management skills, startup capital, business centres like internet café and computer lessons.

Table 4.5.1.2

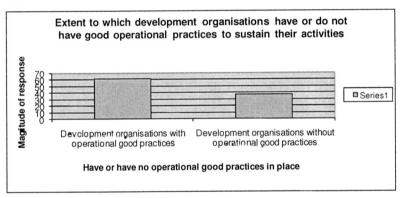

On the other hand, 37.5% of the respondents identified development organisations/ community partnership as an effective strategy in provision of educational delivery and HIV and AIDS mitigation. I should indicate here development organisations having business enterprise feel is a good practice with potential to sustain donor supported activities upon phase out. Even those that see community partnership as a more strategic practice, still feel that business enterprise is a good practice.

Tables 4.5.1.2 and 4.5.1.3 indicate peer responses that development organisations and donor agencies respectively must do to improve impact on HIV mitigation as well as education provision to children and households affected.

Table 4.5.1.2

No	Advice	No of responses	%
1	Community public partnership	2	25
2	IGA and other empowerment activities	4	50
3	Collaboration and networking	1	12.5
4	Need driven by communities	1	12.5
	Total	**8**	**100**

Table 4.5.1.3 further summaries the table 4.5.1.2 in pie chart presentation.

Table 4.5.1.3

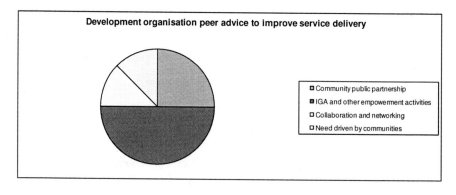

Development organisation peer advice to improve service delivery

□ Community public partnership
■ IGA and other empowerment activities
□ Collaboration and networking
□ Need driven by communities

Table 4.5.1.4 Summary of advices to donor agencies by each of the 8 respondents

No	Advice	No of responses	%
1	Encourage and support economic/business empowerment	1	12.5
2	Should fund long term projects	4	50
3	Enough funds to HIV and educational support	2	25
4	Donor Govt Partnership in infrastructure development	1	12.5
	Total	**8**	**100**

Table 4.5.1.4 above is further summarized in graphical presentation in as shown in table below.

Table 4.5.1.5

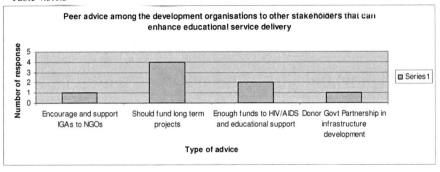

4.5.2 Findings from School Management

Ten out of twelve (10/12) questionnaires administered to schools for school managers were successfully returned. This represents a response rate of 83%. The questionnaire for this category sought to explore the level of service delivery and other administrative aspects from a school's point of view. It also sought to get tips directed at policy makers and sponsoring organizations that can improve on current gaps in the overall programming and service delivery.

In terms of impact, school managers and their guidance teachers indicated that development organisations support a significant number of children with educational requites in their schools. Table 4.5.1.6 presents the total number of children supported by development organisation from eight (8) respondent schools (community, basic and high schools).

Fig 4.5.1.6   Number of children receiving educational support

Name of School	Type of school	sex		Total	% per
		Girls	Boys		School
Gorge Community	Community School	301	300	601	34
Jesus Cares Skills Training	Skills Training	300	230	530	30
Lubi House	Basic School	03	02	05	0.3
Chunga	High School	81	51	132	7.5
Mutambe	Basic School	130	103	233	13
New Chunga	Basic School	01	00	01	0.05
Kamanga	Basic School	20	20	40	2.3
Kamanga Thandizeni	Open Community School	38	18	56	3.2
Chaisa	High School	85	75	155	8.8
Total		**959**	**794**	**1,753**	**100**
Gender Parity %		**55**	**45**	**100**	

This data can be presented in graph indicating the number of children receiving educational support in one of the four (4) categories namely vocational skills, community schooling, high school and basic schooling.

Table 4.5.1.7

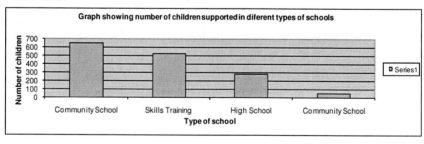

In terms of delivery, 80% of the respondents acknowledge that development organizations contribute significantly to education delivery as well as mitigating impact of HIV and AIDS. In their view, the support given has enabled children from poor and HIV and AIDS affected

55

household access basic and high school education opportunities. In addition, the respondents indicated that HIV and AIDS sensitization initiatives in schools enable children acquire life skills to protect themselves from the pandemic, hence reducing their vulnerability.

However, the other 20% of respondents are of the view that the HIV and AIDS pandemic still cause huge impact on households, resulting into more and more orphaned children. In their view, as long as HIV and AIDS remains a big killer, then the work of development organisations will still have not recorded the desired and sustainable impact.

In terms of sustaining the support they give, only 30% of the respondents were found to have sustainability plans. This has a great challenge because the 70% respondents without sustainability plan is too big a number to be ignored. Imagine the fate of the many children whom they support once this external funding ends. Among the sustainability mechanisms included paying of exam fees for children by schools, and linking them to other sponsors. This response came from school managers. On the other hand, the majority of the development organizations who are apparently responsible for designing interventions do not have sustainability mechanisms.

Administratively, there was a 1:1 response. The respondents who do not face administrative challenges indicated that sponsoring organisations always cooperate and abide by rules and regulations of their schools. On the other hand, the respondents facing administrative challenges also acknowledge the good intentions and significant impact realized sponsoring organisations.

However, some of school management and individual guidance teachers indicated that they face challenges in administering. These may be within and or out side the control of the sponsoring organisations. The following graph shows the types and magnitudes of challenges they face from time to time.

Table 4.5.1.8

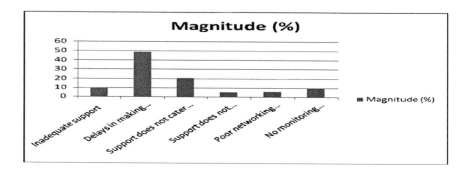

From the graph above, it is evident that school authorities and guidance teachers are faced with challenges especially with regards to timely payments from sponsoring organisations. In addition, schools as intermediaries made a number of observations and suggestions that can improve service delivery to stakeholders. Below is summary of suggestions and % weight against each suggestion that must be incorporated by development organisations to address various challenges faced by school management and guidance teachers.

- Nutritional supplements to children (15%)
- Empower caregivers, guardians and schools with business enterprises since they are closer to their children (38%)
- Continue supporting high school supported graduates to tertiary education (20%)
- Continue with HIV and AIDS sensitization initiatives (21%)
- Impact life skills to children (5%)

To government, below is summary of suggestions that school managers feel can enhance the delivery of educational services to children and also HIV and AIDS mitigation with % weight as against each suggestion.

- Implement practical free basic education (21%)
- Introduce and implement practical free education in high schools (19%)
- Give special priority to children affected by the HIV and AIDS (17%)

- The bursary scheme in tertiary education must be need determined rather than being an entitlement (27%)
- Bursary scheme given to children in government should also extend to community school needy children (8%)
- Training guidance teacher to build their capacity to administer special issues effectively in schools (8%)

4.5.3 Findings from Children as Beneficiaries

With regards to level of education of respondents, 17% of the twenty two (22) respondents were from high schools while the rest 83% are from basic, community and vocational skills training schools. However, I need to indicate also that six (6) respondents from high schools did not return questionnaires.

There were a number of interesting responses on the question that sought to explore the average duration of time respondents have received educational support and overall duration of support. I should also state that some children did not know and or were not sure on this question. Another important finding is that most of the support is project based with an average of 1 to 3 years project duration. In addition, very few (9%) respondents were guaranteed support until they finish Grade 7 and possibly continue in the eighth grade.

Interestingly only two (2) respondents sponsored are assured of educational support till tertiary level, representing another % weight of 9%. On the other hand, two (3) respondents indicated that their sponsors are willing to carry them along till they graduate from being children (up to the age of 18). The question then is what will happen to these children should they turn over 18 years while in high or tertiary school?

Another interesting response came from an HIV and AIDS infected girl who got the sponsorship upon diagnosis of HIV. This is interesting because in most cases, HIV positive children are discriminated against when it comes to accessing essential services such as education. In this case, a development organisation has taken her on with educational support.

In terms of adequacy of support, there were three (3) categories of responses. About 45% of respondents were satisfied with the level of support they receive from the sponsoring organisations. Secondly, 41% respondents were not satisfied with the support they received and suggested requirements that can holistically address the gaps. Lastly, 14% respondents were not sure or did not know.

Though there was no single respondent who indicated the name of another sponsor, dual sponsorship among some of the children in schools does exist. About 27% of respondents mentioned dual support from well wishers such as churches, communities, Christmas education gifts and presents etc. However, 73% indicated that they solely depend on single sponsorship from development organisations.

On sustainability of support, 77% of respondents do not have any potential source of support to sustain their current sponsorships end. Though 14% respondents indicated that they can continue, they all rely on good will of church members and the communities. The remaining 9% are not sure and one respondent did not hesitate to mention that the phase out of the current sponsorship marks the end of his education prospects. In terms of advice to sponsoring organisations, the children suggested a number of critical issues that they feel need to be considered and implemented. Table 4.5.1.10 presents the five (5) major suggestions from the children.

Table 4.5.1.11 is a graphical presentation of the data tabulated in table 4.5.1.9 as a further analysis of the same responses above.

Table 4.5.1.9   Advice to sponsoring organisations to improve education service

No	Response	Frequency	%
1	I do not know	04	18
2	Provide adequate school requirements	04	18
3	Empowering care givers with start up capital for IGAs	10	45
4	Empowering children with IGAs and life skills	03	14
5	Empowering schools with start up capital for IGAs	01	05
	Total	**22**	**100**

Table 4.5.1.10

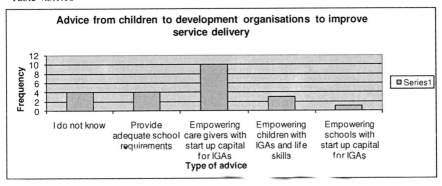

Further, the children had six (6) suggestions that the government need to implement if vulnerable children were to practically enjoy their right to education, even though not justifiable in the Zambian constitution.

These are reflected in fig 4.5.1.13 and graph 4.5.1.14 summarises the key issues that government can do improve on educational service delivery and accessibility by children affected with HIV and AIDS including poverty. Table 4.5.1.13 summaries the type of advice that children feel government must address in order to improve access to educational services by children affected and or infected by HIV and AIDS pandemic

Table 4.5.1.11 Advice from children to government to improve education service

No	Response	Frequency	%
1	I do not know	02	10
2	Develop vocational skills and youth training centres	01	05
3	Target and provide bursaries to vulnerable children	05	23
4	Introduce and implement practical free education to Grade 12	10	45
5	Introduce free education till tertiary level	02	10
6	Increase school places by building new schools	01	05
	Total	22	100

Table 4.5.1.12 Graphical Presentation of table 4.5.1.11

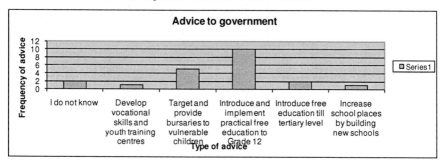

4.5.4 Findings from Donor Agencies

Four (4) donor agencies were sampled to cross-check the information obtained from the development organisations, school management and children. However, only three (3) donor agencies (ILO, Save the Children Norway and CHANGES 2) successfully filled and returned questionnaires. In terms of programming, all of them have HIV interventions that target children and some extent caregivers. The findings further indicate close linkages and relationship between HIV and education accessibility by children (ILO – IPEC, 2007). In addition, all the respondents use education as one of their key strategic models to respond to HIV among children and households.

In terms of coverage, CHANGES 2 supports four (4) development organisations and further gives technical support to government through MoE and specifically to District Education Boards Secretary (DEBS) offices. Among the beneficiary organisations are Family Health Trust (FHT), Copperbelt Health Education Project (CHEP), Forum of Women Educationalist in Zambia (FAWEZA) and Adrakafi.

Secondly, ILO supports three lead partners (Jesus Cares Ministries, Hosanna Mapalo, and Community Youth Concern) who in turn work with locally based partners to provide educational support to children withdrawn and those at risk of entering child labour and exposure to HIV and AIDS pandemic.

Thirdly, Save the Children Norway has similar approach as CHANGES 2 though the former works with MoE through DEBS offices and other development organisations. In terms of duration of support, they all range from 1 year to 3 years on average. With regards to sustainability of projects, the following practices were identified as strategic models that they use to sustain projects to yield impact and continuity, which serve as good practices.

- Use of existing government structures   such as DEBS offices, schools and other structures in the relevant ministries
- Building capacity of implementing agencies, beneficiaries and the community for ownership of the interventions once the external resources end
- Encourage linkages of activities so that when one project phase out , other donors can take over
- Empower caregivers with entrepreneurial skills to run business enterprises to sustain children upon project phase out.

The findings suggest that all interventions must be designed with full participation of key stakeholders at all levels. Communities, children, MoE and other key line ministry staff must be involved at all levels delivery. The intervention must also build the capacity of the community for eventual takeover and ownership.

Further, donors suggest that there is need for collaboration and networking among themselves and other stakeholders doing similar activities to avoid duplication of support and hence, maximise on impact.

4.5.5   Findings from Government As a Respondent

Findings from government were obtained as primary data and secondary literature. Accordingly, government values support and partnership that development organisations and communities play in HIV mitigation and education delivery. The government also commends input of partners in HIV mitigation and support to children and households affected especially that all such efforts supplements government efforts.

To achieve and maintain quality education, MoE provides guidance to development organisations and communities so that they use recommended syllabus and text books. Government indicated that development organisations and communities must involve technocrats from relevant line ministries if impact of interventions were to be achieved. MoE is the custodian of all policies and guidelines that govern education management and delivery such as infrastructure standards, syllabus, curriculum etc.

Similarly, any interventions that seek to reduce the impact of child labour and education must work with both ministry of labour and education. On other hand, the MLSS is the custodian of policies and statutory instruments on child labour and other related matters. The findings show close linkages in that children withdrawn and prevented from HIV induced child labour require reintegration into government and community schools.

Again, MYSCD and MCDSS are other ministries that are cardinal in the implementation and enforcement of government policies on children and education. In addition MYSCD and MCDSS also have child protection policies and social protection mechanisms that seek to improve wellbeing of household income and children such as the Public Welfare Schemes.

Further, it was suggested that donors should have an effective monitoring and tracking mechanism so that the resources given to development organisations and communities reach the intended beneficiaries.

Lastly, the findings from government indicate need for networking and sharing of information on lessons and challenges in HIV mitigation and education delivery. This addresses the possibility of support duplication because the directory can show;

- who is doing what
- to whom,
- where
- with whom,
- for how long and so on.

In short, the government suggests creation of a directory of partners containing all relevant information about what they do and exist for. Accordingly, this can assist them in their planning because the directory can show the areas and population of people not catered for in educational, HIV and other socio-economic projects.

4.6   SUMMARY OF THE CHAPTER

The findings from both literature review and primary sources acknowledge that HIV and AIDS have negative impact on socio-economic set up. Inevitably, this brings into force other factors such as poverty due to reduced household incomes as a result of chronic illness of people. Productive time is lost on account of attending funerals.

In addition, it is evident that development organisations and communities play a critical role in mitigating impact of HIV and AIDS on education. Their passion for assisting the less privileged in society has opened up opportunities for children with little and no hope to remain or start school upon the death of parents and or guardians.

In addition, the impact of HIV and AIDS on individuals and households cannot be addressed by one person or organisation. It requires coordinated fronts and efforts by many players to holistically address the different entry points, spread, impact and coping mechanisms. Worthy mentioning is the important role government plays at policy level. However, the sustainability of all the interventions lies in close collaborations with government and community existing structures. Both desk literature and primary data indicate that provision of educational support services has a number of challenges to implementing agencies and the beneficiaries themselves.

Sustainability of interventions upon project phase out is a very big challenge. Though business enterprise as one of the sustainability strategies, they still face challenges in terms of sourcing adequate capital including the competitiveness of the market.

CHAPTER 5

5.0 DISCUSSION AND INTERPRETATION OF FINDINGS

5.1 INTRODUCTION

In this chapter, the findings presented in Chapter 4 will be discussed, analysed and interpreted according to desk review and primary responses. The discussion and interpretation of findings seek to bring together theoretical and practical relationships of the study variables. The chapter will end with a concise conclusion of major discussion and interpretation of research findings.

5.2 DISCSUSSION AND INTERPRETATION

5.2.1 The General Impact of HIV in Zambia

From the findings presented in Chapter 4, there is significance evidence that there is a relationship between HIV, poverty and loss of socio-economic productivity. In addition, there is also evidence that HIV and poverty affect individual productivity which in turn exerts an impact on income levels (International Federation of the Red Cross (2006 – 2010P4). It does not matter which ever comes first, the end result is that there is a reduction in people's productivity and reduced access to essential household needs such as food, shelter, quality medical care and access to quality education.

In addition, HIV is cited as one of the cause/effect of the increase in the number of orphaned children with little or no care at all. The coming of HIV has among other things brought in the social impact of street children, children working in working in quarries, mines and other hazardous environment including children heading households at a tender age (in most cases even before attaining the age of maturity). These exert budgetary limitation on government and other social service.

5.2.2 Decline in Extended Family Safety Nets

It is unfortunate that once a person is infected with HIV the end result in most cases is death. Moreover, those in productive ages between 15 and 40 years are the hardest hit (UNICEF, 2002). These people, if at all they had children before their demise, leave them at very tender age. They are too young to organise and fend for themselves. Institutionalized orphanages have emerged

65

and but also have problems of sustainability. Those who are not taken in by few extended families and orphanages, have no option but organise themselves into other dangerous survival systems such as prostitution or even working in brothels.

Unfortunately, most of the options expose them further to infection of HIV and other equally dangerous survival methods. Engagement into child labour, living in child headed households, commercial sexual exploitation including working in unsafe homes as domestic workers are some of the survival methods that increase the vulnerability of children to HIV (International Federation of Red Cross, 2006 -1010: P4).

5.2.3   Impact of HIV on Socio-Economic Development
Poverty and HIV also affect children's time to attend school. As a chronic disease, HIV mostly results into death, and children who lose their parents assume roles of breadwinners. Some also take huge responsibility of nursing their chronically ill members of their families. These roles deny them opportunities to attend school. The frequency of HIV related deaths also affects socio-economic productivity because significant time is spent attending to funerals. In such scenarios, there is less productivity and this result into reduced incomes. On the other hand, money is equally required to meet funeral expenses.

5.2.4   Impact of HIV on Education Delivery
HIV affects other parts of delivery of education in the supply chain management. According to Dr. Kanganja, at least 600 teachers die of HIV every year and this affects teaching staff in entire system. This is a significant number, taking into account the amount of resources government spends to train and replace teachers. The teacher to pupil ratio is unpleasant because many schools have fewer teachers than provided for by the establishment. In addition the teacher to pupil contact time ratio is also unpleasant due to chronic illness of teachers.

5.4   IMPACT AND SUSTAINABILITY
5.4.1   Impact of Development Organisation Initiatives in Zambia
From the findings, 75% of the 8 school managers indicate that development organisations support a significant number of children with educational requites in their schools. This is

evident in fig 4.3 presented in Chapter 4. From the 8 schools sampled, 1,753 children receive educational support from development organisations and communities. This number is significant, taking into account that this number of children came from only 8 schools.

. Table 4.5.6 (Chapter 4): Number of children receiving educational support

| Name of School | Type of school | sex | | Total | % per |
		Girls	Boys		School
Gorge Community	Community School	301	300	601	34
Jesus Cares Skills Training	Skills Training	300	230	530	30
Lubi House	Basic School	03	02	05	0.3
Chunga	High School	81	51	132	7.5
Mutambe	Basic School	130	103	233	13
New Chunga	Basic School	01	00	01	0.05
Kamanga	Basic School	20	20	40	2.3
Kamanga Thandizeni	Open Community School	38	18	56	3.2
Chaisa	High School	85	75	155	8.8
Total		959	794	1,753	100
Gender Parity %		55	45	100	

The gender disparity in terms of support of 55% and 45% in favour of girls and boys respectively infers that girls are more affected than boys. ILO-IPEC (2006:P39) suggests that gender equality is very much an issue in relation to HIV especially its links to child labour. Allocating of resources and chances to access schooling are tilted towards boys than girls. This leaves girls more disadvantaged than boys but the % of 55% and 45% in favour of girls to boys can assist to harmonize the intervention.

5.4.2 Effectiveness in Delivery of Support Services

The findings in chapter 4 show that 80% out of 8 school respondents acknowledge the effectiveness of development organisations in education service delivery. They also acknowledge similar effectiveness in addressing the impact of HIV and AIDS. Their ability to target the real vulnerable children in society gives development organisations a more competitive edge than government service delivery methodology. The support enables children from poor and HIV and AIDS affected households to equally access basic and high school education. The HIV and AIDS initiatives have increased provision and dissemination of adequate and accurate information about HIV and AIDS in schools. This has reduced stigma and discrimination against children infected and those from households affected by HIV and AIDS. Through sensitization, some myths like how the HIV virus spreads have been corrected. This has reduced isolation and exclusion of affected children from the rest of the children. Ultimately, there is reduction in children dropping out of school on grounds of failing to cope with stigma and discrimination.

However, more is still required to be done especially in rural areas where stigma and discrimination are still rampant. Denis Wood indicates that children in schools in Western Province of Zambia are more comfortable to relate with a child whose parent died of suspected witchcraft than one whose parent died of HIV related illness. Though 20% of 8 school respondents feel that development organisations have not recorded significant progress to halt the spread and impact of HIV, significant improvements have been made in this area. HIV is a multifaceted pandemic that affects the different aspects of life. As a result, it is not expected to be addressed with much ease.

5.4.3 Beneficiary Perception on Support

Of the 22 beneficiaries, 45% are satisfied with the amount of support they receive, 41% respondents are not satisfied while 14% are not sure or did not know. This shows that the magnitude of support is adequate. Probably, development organisations need to explain to children about resource limitation, which is shared among many children in need of support. It is possible that children who felt unsatisfied with support expected more than what can be given.

5.4.4 Sustainability Plans beneficiary

The findings in Chapter 4 indicate that only 30% out of 8 development organisation respondents have sustainability plans. This is a small number, considering the number of children currently supported. This is worrying when one looks at the sustainability upon end of external support.

On the other hand, the remaining 70% out of 8 development respondents without any plans of sustaining their support is too big to ignore.

Table 5.4.4.1

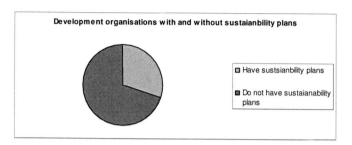

In addition, even the 30% of with sustainability mechanisms may not practically be sustainable. Only few school respondents indicated practical sustainability which includes schools paying of exam fees for children once they stop receiving support. The other mechanism seeks to link the children to other sponsors still depends on the availability of external resources, which may come or may not come.

On the other hand, 77% out of 22 beneficiaries do not have any potential source of support once their current sponsorships end. Though 14% respondents indicated that they can continue, they all rely on the goodwill of church members and communities. The remaining 9% are not sure. This shows a huge challenge associated with dependence on external aid. As was seen in the presentation in chapter 4, most of the support are donor driven and have average life span of 1 to 3 years.

In the absence of sustainability plans, children are temporarily in school. When their current support ends, they automatically go back to their former vulnerable situations. In such scenarios, therefore, the support cannot be said to have addressed the educational needs of these children. Ultimately, HIV still finds an entry point through child labour, commercial sexual exploitation, and unsafe domestic work among others.

5.5 SUMMARY OF THE CHAPTER

In this chapter, discussion and interpretation of the findings were done based on research findings presented in chapter 4. Tabulations and percentages (%) were used to ascertain the magnitude and impact of the study variables. In brief, the discussion and interpretation of findings show that HIV and AIDS have impact on the entire socio-economy and specifically on children's access to education. In addition, other factors like poverty, child labour, orphanhood and others contribute towards the spread and impact of HIV and AIDS among children. These may cause or are result of HIV depending on the cycle of infection.

In short therefore, HIV and AIDS individually and or collectively affect socio-economic productivity. This also leads to reduction in household income. The reduction in income affects purchasing power of households. Ultimately, households affected by HIV and AIDS have no ability to pay for essential basic needs which include education, food, shelter and clothing.

As a chronic disease, HIV and AIDS affect people's contribution in productive work in the labour market of the economy. A lot of time is lost when they are ill and also attending funerals of deceased relatives, workmates including church mates. In addition, significant resources are spent to meet funeral relate costs.

From the discussion, it is evident that development organisations play a critical role in mitigating impact of HIV and AIDS on education. This is evident from a big number of children supported by just 8 development organization which participated in the research. It should be noted that addressing the impact of HIV require coordinated fronts and efforts by all key players and beneficiaries.

In addition, the involvement of all stakeholders at all levels of intervention management builds their capacity to prepare them for eventual takeover. This also guarantees the sustainability of intervention especially with strong collaboration and coordination with existing government and community structures.

Sustainability still remains a big challenge in managing externally supported interventions. A lot of uncertainty still exist as to what happens when donor time specific aid end. Though empowerment of caregivers in entrepreneurial skills was identified as a potential sustainability strategy, practical implementation has a number of challenges. It is not ease for a small scale entrepreneur to raise adequate capital, produce competitive goods and services better than those produced by big competitors. As a result, most of the entrepreneurs lack markets to sell their produce and end up being exploited due to lack of market information. Others opt to sell at exploitative prices knowingly because they do not have the capacity to ferry their goods and service to competitive markets (ILO-IPEC Peer Review Report, 2008: 21).

Both potential and currently used good practices were also discussed in the chapter. These included the use of existing government and community structures, networking and collaboration among development organisations and donors, empowerment of caregivers with business enterprise skills , practical implementation of free education in basic as well as in high school and among others.

However, government as front seat driver for policies that safe guard rights of children, there is need to domesticate all provision of UN CRC, and ACWRC to make education a justifiable right in the national constitution. In addition, the government needs to double her efforts towards realisation of MDGs benchmarks by 2015. Lastly, basic education in Zambia is not free because it has a lot of related costs.

CHAPTER 6

6.0   CONCLUSION AND RECOMMENDATIONS
6.1   INTRODUCTION

In this chapter, the conclusions of research findings are summarized. Secondly, some major action points and recommendations of the research to various stakeholders are also discussed.

6.2   FACTORS PREVENTING ELIMINATION OF HIV PANDEMIC
6.2.1   Household Poverty Levels

Various documented desk literature indicate that poverty is linked directly as well as indirectly to the spread of the HIV and AIDS pandemic in society. This is because inadequate household income lead to chronic illness and deaths of breadwinners, inevitably affects children's access, and completion of basic education. Therefore, households with inadequate incomes become vulnerable to impact of HIV and AIDS especially when breadwinners become chronically ill and or die. According to the Living Conditions Monitoring Survey of 2004, Lusaka District accounted for 57.8% of the total number of vulnerable children affected by HIV and AIDS (CSO, 2004). This is high and it goes without saying that children from these households lack access to education, food, clothing and other basic essentials like healthcare in Lusaka District.

6.2.2   Inadequate Social Protection Safety Nets

Prior to emergence of HIV and AIDS, there were no terms as orphaned and other vulnerable children as well as child headed households because extended families had strong coping mechanisms to take in children left upon deaths of parents and other breadwinners. However, the spread of HIV and AIDS and its socio-economic impact in the last 25 years has destroyed the once strong extended family safety nets and social cohesion networks. As a result, children are no longer left in the hands of extended family.

6.2.3   Effects of Privatisation on Household Incomes

The privatisation policy that Zambia embraced in the early 1990s entails a shift from socially regulated to market-driven economy. The immediate effects of the new economic management among others were restructuring and down sizing of companies through redundancies and retrenchments. The effect has been mass unemployment because new company and businesses owners wanted few but competent staff establishments.

6.2.4 Children as Caregivers

When guardians/parents become chronically ill, particularly in poor homes, children come under stress in different ways and this continues for the rest of their childhood. Some take up heavy burdens to nurse chronically ill family members and because of this; they inevitably forgo opportunities to attend school.

6.2.5 Impact of Stigma and Discrimination

Apart from the loss of parents due to HIV and AIDS related illness, many children also suffer stigma and discrimination from their peers in schools and this also extends to homes and communities they li.ve Unfortunately, this affects children's level of interaction with peer in class and in recreation events. In most cases, the majority of these children fail to cope with and end up hating school and completely drop out on account of rejection.

6.2.6 Impact of HIV on Teaching Staff

HIV affects exchange of knowledge between teachers and children. Teachers are also prone to contracting HIV and this affects their teaching capability because of chronic illness, leading to absenteeism as well as ultimate deaths. In such scenarios, there is limited and even no interaction between affected teachers and the children. The reduction in teacher to pupil interaction affects the delivery and as a result, children miss out on access to quality education.

6.2.7 Decline in Extended Family and others Social Safety Nets

The decline in extended family safety nets leave orphaned children without parental care and support. They take up options which further expose them to infection of HIV due to dangerous survival methods such as child labour, children working in brothels including those working in unsafe homes as domestic workers.

6.3   GOOD PRACTICES AND THEIR EFFECTIVENESS

A good practice is strategy that has been tested, proved and or has the potential to produce desired results. Some of the good practices identified in the research are highlighted.

6.3.1   Strengthening the Social Protection and Bursary Schemes

The Public Welfare Assistance Scheme (PWAS) is a good and effective government instrument that improves household income provided that there is adequate funding to address poverty and HIV and AIDS households. Secondly, practical implementation of free basic education by government can be a good practice. In its current form, education is far from being free. Thirdly, a strengthened bursary scheme in tertiary education which is more targeting and need determined can improve education opportunities for vulnerable children.

6.3.2   Empowerment of Caregivers with Entrepreneurial Skills

Since the spread and impact of HIV and AIDS is linked to poverty, empowerment of caregivers with IGAs and other business skills improves the household incomes. This income can sustain children supported with education requites when external funding from NGOs end. It can also be used to scale up and reach huge numbers of orphaned children currently in need of financial and materials support (ILO-IPEC Peer Review Report, 2008: 12).

6.3.3   Working with Existing Government and Community Structures

The use of existing government and community structures is viewed as a good practice for project impact and sustainability. This is so because government and community structures remain even when external support ends. In addition, community schools are a good practice that has evolved and embraced in many Zambian communities. Similarly, once communities are technically empowered, they can contribute to reducing the HIV impact.

6.3.4   Involvement of Stakeholders

The involvement of communities and beneficiaries guarantees community ownership and takeover of a project when external support ends. This can be realized by involvement of stakeholders at all levels of project management. It should also be realized that children have the right to contribute and participate fully on issues that affect them. Therefore, stakeholders must take keen interest to develop the capacity of children and over a period of time, they are able to participate fully. If it is an HIV project, let the children as beneficiaries take an active role. Similarly, if it is an educational project, let the children get involved to contribute how they want the services delivered to meet their needs.

6.3.5 Strengthening the Extended Family Safety Nets

The increase in the capacity of extended family can reduce children's vulnerability and their exposure to HIV through survival and coping mechanisms. This reduce the number of children engaged into child labour, commercial sex exploitation, child headed households, children working in unsafe domestic households and among others.

6.3.6 Effective Networking and Linkages among Stakeholders

Networking and collaboration provides a platform for people doing similar or related things to share and learn from one another. This creates linkages and common understating on issues of common interest. It also reduces possibilities of duplicating support to same beneficiaries. Networking and linkages among stakeholders maximise impact because of synergy and coordination.

6.3.7 Private Sector Corporate Social Responsibility

Corporate social responsibility is a good practice that corporations must continue to develop and embrace. In Zambia, Celtel in partnerships with other corporations, they demonstrated how the private sector individually and collectively can change people's lives. The Touching Lives Initiative must be replicated by other corporations. In addition, MTN's Africa Challenge is another private sector initiative that has contributed to academic knowledge for students from tertiary education institutions in Africa.

In addition, the HIV workplace policies are good practices that directly and indirectly reduce the spread and impact of HIV pandemic. Once HIV is reduced at work places, employees' vulnerability, infection, chronic illness and death will be reduced. This also reduces the frequency of children being orphaned by the death of parents and guardians. With employees in good health and in employment, productivity and household income remain unaffected.

Ultimately, households will afford all basic essentials such nutritious food, shelter, education and healthcare.

6.4   IMPACT AND SUSTAINABILITY

75% research findings show significant evidence that development organisations contribute to children's access to education. In addition, the said findings show that 1,753 children received educational support from development organisations and communities. This number is significant, taking into account that the said number of children came from only 8 schools in selected townships in the Lusaka district of Zambia.

In spite of the aforementioned impact, development organisations do not have sustainability plans for children they support. As evidenced by the research findings in Chapter 4 only 30% respondents indicated that they had sustainability plans and this is too small a number, considering the number of children currently supported. This worries beneficiaries, donors and development organisations with regards to the fate of the many children upon project phase out. The remaining 70% respondents don not have any sustainability plans.

On the other hand, even 30% who indicated that they have sustainability mechanisms, only schools that indicated practical sustainability where schools must pay exam fees for children upon phase out of external support. However, the other mechanism that seeks to link the children to other sponsors still depends on availability of external resources. In addition, 77% out of 22 children do not have any potential source of support once their current sponsorships end as indicated in table 6.4.1 below.

Table 6.4.1

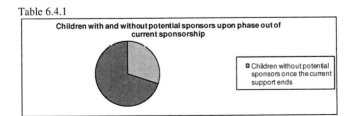

6.5   RESEARCH CONCLUSION

From the findings and discussions, it is evident that HIV coupled with poverty and child labor affects children's chances to basic education. These factors have far reaching impacts. Mostly available coping mechanisms are equally bad and do not promote and protect the rights of such children.

Prior to emergence of HIV, there were no OVCs as well as child headed households because extended families had strong coping mechanisms to take in children left upon deaths of parents and breadwinners. However, the spread of HIV and its socio-economic impact in the last 25 years have destroyed the once strong extended family safety nets and social cohesion networks. As a result, children are no longer left under the care of extended families.

However, it should be pointed out here that the change in social coping mechanisms does not mean that all children found in vulnerable situations do not have next of keens to take charge of their affairs. The scenario is that there is an increase in the number of parents dying and therefore, the surviving family members are too constrained to take in more orphaned children into their households. Unfortunately, this lack of extended family and other coping mechanisms make orphaned children extremely vulnerable. Denis Wood suggests that the prevalence and severity of HIV and AIDS fuels the dramatic increase in levels of child mortality rates and this has further resulted into the increase in the number of orphans (Save the Children Sweden, 2008).

HIV also has direct negative impact on schools attendance for children with chronically ill parents/breadwinners or those who have lost their parents. This has led to increased demand on educational support from development and others. Further, HIV undermines the Zambia's chances towards achieving the 8 MDGs by 2015 (Human Development Report 2007).

On the other hand, poverty also contributes to the spread of HIV which further affects household income. In addition, HIV and poverty affect individual productivity which in turn exerts negative impact on household income levels. The death of a breadwinner in a family as a result of HIV reduces the surviving family's access to essential household needs including education.

77

6.6   RECOMMENDATIONS

Below is a summary of key action points and recommendations for stakeholder to mitigate impact of HIV on education of affected children. They are classified into short, medium and long term.

6.6.1   Short term

- Under part 3 of the Zambian constitution (the bill of rights), the right to education should be justiciable in the courts of law if violated by the government or any other stakeholder. Once this is done, it may increase responsibility upon the duty bearers who are entrusted to ensuring that policies, school places and learning requisites are made available to children. It is hoped that the National Constitutional Conference (NCC) currently reviewing the constitution could have a look into at this report.

- As well articulated in the Fifth National Development Plan (FNDP), government should embark on transforming the plans by addressing HIV and other cross cutting issues which affect educational delivery to make the plan more responsive to current needs of vulnerable children.

- Government must allocate adequate resources to implement and strengthen HIV policies in the ministries.

- Government must increase budgetary allocation to Public Assistance and Welfare Schemes to address poverty, HIV and other socio-economic factors.

- Development organisations must work with existing government and community structures when designing and implementing development initiatives for greater impact and sustainability.

- Donors should support both development organisations and caregivers with applicable means of empowerment such as business skills to sustain operations and reach huge numbers of orphaned children currently in need of financial and materials support.

- Stakeholders implementing initiatives involving children must take practical steps to involve and consult children

- Stakeholders must network and collaborate with one another to increase linkages and synergy on issues of common interest. This also reduces possibilities of duplicating support to same beneficiaries and maximise of impact due to synergy.

78

6.6.2 Medium term

- The Zambian government must domesticate international treaties and conventions (UN CRC and ACRWC) to enhance children's access to basic human rights.
- Government and other partners must invest in school infrastructural development through construction of new schools and renovating old schools to carter for the growing demand for school places resulting from increase in the population.
- More HIV sensitization initiatives must be done in communities, schools, colleges and universities to reduce stigma and discrimination against pupils and students who could be infected or those lost their family members due to HIV.
- Government must practically implement free basic education in both high school and tertiary education (Mukuka Lombe etal 2004). Secondly, the bursary scheme in tertiary education must be need determined so that only financially disadvantaged students are supported.
- More private sector corporations must continue implementing corporate social responsibility to reach out children in need of educational and other socio-economic needs.

6.6.3 Long term

- The international community must devise strong monitoring mechanisms on state party's commitment and progress towards implementation of agreed treaties and conventions (UN CRC, MDGs, and ACRWC).
- Government must finalise the development of a National Plan of Action on child labour to facilitate the elimination of worst forms of child labour by 2016.
- Government must continue encouraging partnership with other stakeholders in education delivery
- Employers from all sectors must support HIV workplace policies and good practices to reduce spread and impact including stigma and discrimination.

APPENDICES

Appendix No. 4.2.1.1

Dear Respondent,

Your organization has been chosen by the researcher to be part of a sample of ten (10) development organisations that may assist him to critically analyze of effectiveness and sustainability of educational models in mitigating impact of HIV on Children in Zambia. *A Case Study Conducted in 4 Communities in Lusaka District.*

Kindly assist by providing answers to the questions in this questionnaire by ticking and or providing brief explanation where applicable. You are further assured that the information being sought and identity **shall be** treated with professional confidentiality.

Thank you for your time and anticipated cooperation.

Peter Matimba

....

Category A: Questionnaire for development organizations

1.   Name of development organization...

2.   Position of respondent in the organization:...

3 (i) Does your organization have HIV interventions targeting children?

     a)   Yes   b)   No

3 (ii). Is education support among the models your organization use to manage the impact of HIV among children (a)   Yes   (b) No

4 (i) From your organization's strategic and operational point of view, is there any relationship between HIV and children's access to education?

a)   Yes   b)   No

4 (ii) Explain your answer in 4 (i)

i

....

....

....

5(i).　Do think boys and girls equally affected by impact of HIV in terms of access to educational opportunities?

a)　Yes　　　　　　　b)　No?

5(ii).　Why is it so?...

....

....

5 (iii) Which of the following group does your organization support?

(a)　Girls only　　(b) Boys only　(c) both girls and boys

5 (iv).　In terms of age, which is your target age group?

(a)　Below 7 years (b)　7 to 18 years (c)　Above 18 years

6 (i)　What type of educational support service do you provide?

(a)　Pre and nursery school

(b)　Basic formal education (primary level)

(c)　Non-formal (vocational skills)

(d)　Secondary education

(e)　Tertiary (colleges and university)

(f)　Others, kindly Explain

....

....

6 . Any special reason why your organization's interventions are lined in categories 5(i) and 6(i)?

....

....

7(i).　What strategic model does your organization use in providing educational support services to children?

(a)　Paying school fees and other school requisites

(b)　Capacity building for teachers and their school governance boards (Parents Teachers' Associations)

(c)　School infrastructure development

(d)   Others (kindly explain)

....

....

8 (i)   Do you think it is advisable for development organisations to venture into economic empowerment and other businesses in addition to their core social service provision as a means to sustain their activities?   (a)   Yes   (b) No

8 (ii)   Give   reasons   for   the   answer   in   8(i)

....

....

9. Mention any good strategic and operational practices that your organization has developed and or is developing in order to address sustainability of your support towards educational needs of children currently supported?

....

....

10 (i)   Do you think the type of support you have given so far has brought sustained impact on children's access to education and addressing the HIVS impact?

(a)   Yes   (b)   No

10 (ii)   Explain your answer in question 10 (i) above?

....

....

....

11.   From your experience in providing educational support services and or addressing impact of HIV among children, what advice would you give to;

(i)   Other development organisations if their support were to be have sustained impact?

....

....

....

(ii)   Donors if their financial support were to have sustained impact on your programming and the children's access to education?

Appendix No. 4.2.1.2

Dear Respondent,

You are have been chosen by the researcher to be part of a sample of twenty five (25) respondents that researcher to critically analyze of effectiveness and sustainability of educational models in mitigating impact of HIV on Children in Zambia. *A Case Study Conducted in 4 Communities in Lusaka District.*

Kindly assist by providing answers to the questions in this questionnaire by ticking and or providing brief explanation where applicable. You are further assured that the information being sought and identity **shall be** treated with professional confidentiality Kindly assist by providing answers to the questions in this questionnaire by ticking and or providing brief explanation where applicable. You are further assured that the information being sought and identity **shall** be treated with professional confidentiality.

Thank you for your time and cooperation.

Thank you for your time and anticipated cooperation.

Peter Matimba

....

Category B: Questionnaires for the Beneficiaries Children

1.   Name of respondent:..

2.   Age   ....

3.   Sex   (a)   Girl   (b)   Boy

4.   Name of school or institution..

5.   Grade or year of study...

6.   Name of the sponsoring organisations? ....

7.   What kind of educational support do you get from the organization mentioned in question 6 above?

       (i)   Paying for school fees

v

(ii)   Buying scholastic materials (books, pencils, pens etc)

(iii)   Buying uniforms and shoes

(iv)   Others, kindly specify

....

....

....

8 (i)   How long have you being receiving educational support mentioned 7?.................

8 (ii). How long will the above educational support last?..

9 (i).   Does the support you receive from the organization in question 6 enough to cover your basic educational needs?

(a)   Yes   (b)   No

9 (iii) If the answer above is No, what would you want your sponsoring organization in provide in order to meet your basic educational requirements?

....

....

....

10 (i). Do you get any support from other organizations, church and or community in addition to what you mentioned in question 7 above?

(a)   Yes   (b)   No

10 (ii). If yes, what type of support do you get?

....

....

....

11(i). Once the support you are currently getting end, do you expect another source of support in order for you to continue your education?

(a)   Yes   (b)   No

11 (ii).   If yes, where do you expect to get this support?

....

....

12(i)   What should sponsoring organizations do in order to provide long lasting educational (sustainable) support so that the children they support complete their education without any problems?

....

....

....

....

12(ii). What should Government do in order to allow children without money to equally access to and complete their education?

....

....

....

Dear Respondent,

Your ministry has been chosen by the researcher to be part of a sample of four (04) respondent policy makers that may assist the researcher critically analyze of effectiveness and sustainability of educational models in mitigating impact of HIV on Children in Zambia. *A Case Study Conducted in 4 Communities in Lusaka District.*

Kindly assist by providing answers to the questions in this questionnaire by ticking and or providing brief explanation where applicable. You are further assured that the information being sought and identity **shall be** treated with professional confidentiality. Kindly assist by providing answers to the questions in this questionnaire by ticking and or providing brief explanation where applicable. You are further assured that the information being sought is and identity **shall** be treated with professional confidentiality.

Thank you for your time and anticipated cooperation.

Peter Matimba

....

Part C: Government: (MCDSS, MLSS, MSYCD and MOE)[1]

1. Name of Ministry...

2. Title of the respondent..

3. Department..

4. What is your view with regards to participation of development agencies in provision of educational support services to children affected by HIV and those from economically disadvantaged households?

   ....

   ....

---

[1] MCDSS – Ministry of Community development and Social Services, MLSS represents Ministry of Labour and Social Security, MSYCD represents Ministry of Sports, Youth and Child development and MOE represents Ministry of Education

5. What role does your ministry play to ensure that development organisations provide quality and sustained educational support and above all that the approach does not compromise with government set standards?

....

....

....

6. What suggestions would you propose to donors to ensure that their financial support towards education of children affected with HIV and those from economically disadvantaged households achieve the desired impact and sustainability to supported children in Zambia?

....

....

....

7. What suggestions would you propose to development organisations so that they design sustainable educational models that would effectively respond to educational needs of children affected by HIV and those from economically disadvantaged households in Zambia?

....

....

....

Dear Respondent,

Your school has been chosen by the researcher to be part of a sample of fifteen (15) schools to assist the researcher to critically analyze of effectiveness and sustainability of educational models in mitigating impact of HIV on Children in Zambia. *A Case Study Conducted in 4 Communities in Lusaka District.*

Kindly assist by providing answers to the questions in this questionnaire by ticking and or providing brief explanation where applicable. You are further assured that the information being sought and identity **shall be** treated with professional confidentiality. Kindly assist by providing answers to the questions in this questionnaire by ticking and or providing brief explanation where applicable. You are further assured that the information being sought and identity **shall** be treated with professional confidentiality.

Thank you for your time and anticipated cooperation.

Peter Matimba

....

Category D: Questionnaires for School Management

1. Name of school or institution ....

2. Position of respondent ....

3. Number of development organisations providing educational support to children at your school?...........................

4. Number of children being supported by the organisations mentioned in Question 3?
    (a) ....Girls   (b)............ Boys   (c)...............Total

5. What kind of educational support do the organisations provide to the children at your school?
    (i)   Paying for their school fees
    (ii)   Buying scholastic materials (books and or pencils etc)
    (iii)   Buying uniforms and shoes

(iv)   Others, kindly specify

…………………………………………………………………………………………………

………..…………………………………………………………………………………………

…………………………………………………………………………………………………

6 (i) Do you have any administrative problems and challenges with children supported by organisations at your school?   (a)   Yes   (b)   No

6 (ii). Explain the answer in 6 (i)

…………………………………………………………………………………………………

…………………………………………………………………………………………………

…………………………………………………………………………………………………

7(i). Do you have any administrative problems and challenges with organisations supporting children at your school?   (a)   Yes   (b)   No

7(ii). Explain the answer in 8(i)

…………………………………………………………………………………………………

…………………………………………………………………………………………………

…………………………………………………………………………………………………

8 (i)   Do you think the type of support given by the organisations have improved children's access to education at your school?

(a)   Yes   (b)   No

9 (ii)   Explain your answer in question 8 (i) above?

…………………………………………………………………………………………………

…………………………………………………………………………………………………

…………………………………………………………………………………………………

10 (i). As a school, do you have any means of ensuring that children currently receiving educational support from organisations continue even after the support they receive comes to an end?

(a)   Yes   (b)   No

10 (ii).   If yes, kindly explain?

…………………………………………………………………………………………………

………………..…………………………………………………………………………………

…………………………………………………………………………………………………

11. What suggestions can you make to:

(i)   Organisations so that their support is long lasting and also effectively address the HIV among children?

....

....

....

(ii) Government so that children affected by HIV and those from economically disadvantaged households practically access and complete their education like the rest of children?

....

....

....

Appendix No. 4.2.1.5

Dear Respondent,

Your agency has been chosen by the researcher to be part of a sample of four (04) donor agencies that may assist him to critically analyze effectiveness and sustainability of educational models in mitigating impact of HIV on Children in Zambia. *A Case Study Conducted in 4 Communities in Lusaka District.*

Kindly assist by providing answers to the questions in this questionnaire by ticking and or providing brief explanation where applicable. You are further assured that the information being sought and identity **shall be** treated with professional confidentiality. Kindly assist by providing answers to the questions in this questionnaire by ticking and or providing brief explanation where applicable. You are further assured that the information and identity shall be treated with professional confidentiality.

Thank you for your time and anticipated cooperation.

Peter Matimba

....

Category E: Questionnaire for development organizations

1.   Name of donor..

2 (i).   Name of response..

2 (ii)   Does your agency have HIV intervention targeting children?

a)   Yes   b)   No

3 (ii).   Is education support among the models your agency use to manage the impact of HIV among children (a)   Yes   (b) No

4(i)   From your agency's point of view, is there any relationship between HIV and children's access to education?

a)   Yes   b)   No

4(ii)   Kindly give a brief explanation to your answer above

....

....

....

5(i). How many organisations or partners do you support to contribute towards the education of children in Zambia?

5 (ii). Kindly provide their names if possible

....

....

....

5(iii). Which of the following group does your agency target?

        (a)   Girls only   (b) Boys only (c) both girls and boys

5(iv). In terms of age, which is your target age group?

(a)   Below 7 years (b)   7 to 18 years (c)   Above 18 years

6 (i)   What category of educational support service do you provide?

  (a) Pre and nursery school

  (b) Basic formal education (primary level)

  (c) Non-formal (vocational skills)

  (d) Secondary education

  (e) Tertiary (colleges and university)

  (f) Others, kindly Explain.

6 (ii) Any special reason why your organization's interventions are lined in categories 5(i) and 6(i)?

....

....

....

7(i). What strategic model does your agency prefer so that your partner organisations enhance children access quality education?

(a)   Paying school fees and other school requisites

(b)   Capacity building for teachers and their school governance boards

(c)   School infrastructure development

(d)   Supporting advocacy activities on education through engagement with policy makers

(e)   Others, (kindly explain)

....

....

....

7 (ii)   What measures as an agency do you put in place to ensure that the supported children continue in schools once your support to the organisations phase-out?...

....

....

8 (I) Do you think Economic empowerment and other businesses are options for development organisations to sustain their activities in addition to their core social service provision? (a)

Yes   (b) No

8 (ii)   Give   reasons   for   the   answer   in   8(i)

....

....

....

9. Mention any strategic and or operational practices that your agency has developed and or is developing in order to address sustainability of your support towards educational needs of children currently supported including those equally at risk?

....

....

....

10(i)   Do you think the type of support you have given to partner organisations so far has brought sustained impact on children's access to education and addressing the HIV impact?

(a)   Yes   (b)   No

10(ii)   Explain your answer in question 10 (i) above?

....

....

....

11. From your experience in providing educational support services and or addressing impact of HIV among children, what advice would you give to;

(i) Other donor agencies if their support were to have sustained impact?

....

....

....

(ii) Development organizations they support to design and develop sustainable educational support services to children?

....

....

....

BIBLIOGRAPHY

Best and Khan etal (2003), <u>Research in Education</u>, 7th Edition, Prentice Hall of India, Chicago, USA.

ACRWC (2002), <u>African Charter on the Rights and Welfare of a Child</u>, Addis Ababa, Ethiopia

Beyani C, (2008), <u>Advancement of Children's Rights and the Education</u> Budget, (SCS Office, Lusaka, Zambia)

Care International (2003), <u>Telling our stories: - A tool to help children deal with loss, grief and transition</u>, Lusaka, Zambia

Carmody, B (2004), <u>Evolution of Education in Zambia</u>, Mission Press Ndola, Zambia

Chanda, C: <u>Times of Zambia</u>, 9th May 2008

CHAGNES 2 <u>Project Update</u> for 2005 to 2009, Lusaka, Zambia

Chika G.U (2007), Issues and challenges in the care of HIV and AIDS orphans: case study of Enugu, Nigeria

CIC, <u>Bulletin Up Date</u>, (2007), Lusaka, Zambia

07), Lusaka, Zambia

CSO, (2001), <u>Demographic Health Survey</u> (1997-2001)

CSO, (2004), <u>Living Conditions Monitoring Survey</u>, GRZ, Lusaka, Zambia

CSO, (2005), <u>Zambia Demographic Health Survey</u>, GRZ, Lusaka, Zambia

CSO, (2007), <u>Human Development Report</u> (2007)

CSO, (2005), <u>ILO-IPEC Supported Child Labour Survey Report</u>, GRZ, Lusaka, Zambia

Denis Wood, (SCS, 2008), <u>Social Protection and Children's in Zambia</u>, JCTR, Lusaka, Zambia

Doek, E, J (2007), Paper presentation on response of professionals in the care and treatment of children in HIV era, Kampala, Uganda

Donahue and Williamson, (1999), Firelight Foundation,

Firelight Foundation (2003-2004), Santa Cruz, CA 95060, USA

Gwaba, E, (SCS, 2008), Research on Assessment of Children's Accessibility to Quality
Education in Zambia

International Federation of the Red Cross (2006 – 2010), Raising to the Challenge, Southern
Africa HIV and AIDS Program.

ILO-IPEC (2008), Peer Review Report for Partners implementing HIV and AIDS Induced Child
Labour in Zambia

ILO-IPEC (2007), Working Paper on the Nature and Extent of Child Trafficking in Zambia

Parcel etal (2005), Planning Health Promotions Programs; - An Interventional, Mapping
Approach, (1st Edition), Published by Jose Bass, San Francisco, Canada

Phiri, G, Times of Zambia, May 9 2008

UN CRC (1989), United Nations Convention on the Right of a Child, Geneva, Switzerland

UNGASS (United Nations General Assembly Special Report on AIDS) Report for Zambia, 2008

UNICEF, (2004), A work book on what Religious leaders can do about HIV and AIDS, Action
for Children and young people.

UNICEF (2002), African's Orphaned Generation, Geneva, Switzerland

MCDSS, HIV and AIDS Policy, GRZ, Lusaka, Zambia

Milima A, (2007), Implication of Direct Budget Support Paper on Zambia Presentation, Ibis
Garden Lodge, Chisamba, Zambia

Mukuka Lombe etal (2004), Zambia's Commitment to Children's Rights, the Budget
Perspective, Lusaka, Zambia

MoE (2007), Educational Bulletin, GRZ, Lusaka, Zambia

MoE, (1996), National Educational Policy, GRZ, Lusaka, Zambia

MoE (2007), Strategic Framework for Community Schools for 2007-2010, GRZ, Lusaka, Zambia

MYSCD (2006), National Child Policy GRZ, Lusaka, Zambia

SCS, (2005), Situational Analysis on Children's Rights in Zambia, Lusaka, Zambia

Save the Children UK, (2007), Child Rights Programming, Lusaka, Zambia

Swanpoel, (1998), Community Capacity Building; a Guide for Field Workers and Community leaders, Oxford University Press, South Africa

Times of Zambia May 9, 2008)

World Population Foundation Report (2005), Amsterdam, The Netherlands

Biolgraphy

PETER is a Business Development Consultant, born on 31st October, 1976 in Chief Sianjalika, Zambia. He started Primary Education at Sianzala in 1984, Seconadry Education at Chikankata (1991) and Hilcrest (1993). Peter holds an MBA from Cavendish University (2008) and BBA from Copperbelt University, Zambia (2002). Peter intends to pursue law.

Username: matimba_1@yahoo.co.uk
Password: 6eb6ced84611

Project 28695

VDM publishing house ltd.

Scientific Publishing House

offers

free of charge publication

of current academic research papers, Bachelor´s Theses, Master's Theses, Dissertations or Scientific Monographs

If you have written a thesis which satisfies high content as well as formal demands, and you are interested in a remunerated publication of your work, please send an e-mail with some initial information about yourself and your work to *info@vdm-publishing-house.com.*

Our editorial office will get in touch with you shortly.

VDM Publishing House Ltd.
Meldrum Court 17.
Beau Bassin
Mauritius
www.vdm-publishing-house.com

Printed by
Schaltungsdienst Lange o.H.G., Berlin